Fresh Air, Clean Water

Our Right to a Healthy Environment

ORCA
Think

*Question, connect and take action to become better citizens
with a brighter future. Now that's smart thinking!*

Fresh Air,
Clean Water

Our Right to a Healthy
Environment

Megan Clendenan

illustrated by Julie McLaughlin

ORCA BOOK PUBLISHERS

Published in Canada and the United States in 2022 by Orca Book Publishers.
orcabook.com

Library and Archives Canada Cataloguing in Publication
Title: Fresh air, clean water: our right to a healthy environment / Megan Clendenan; illustrated by Julie McLaughlin.
Names: Clendenan, Megan, 1977– author. | McLaughlin, Julie, 1984– illustrator.
Description: Series statement: Orca think | Includes bibliographical references and index.
Identifiers: Canadiana (print) 20210168048 | canadiana (EBOOK) 20210168056 |
ISBN 9781459826793 (hardcover) | ISBN 9781459826809 (PDF) | ISBN 9781459826816 (EPUB)
Subjects: LCSH: Environmental health—Citizen participation—Juvenile literature. | LCSH: Human rights advocacy—Citizen participation—Juvenile literature. | LCSH: Environmentalism—Citizen participation—Juvenile literature. | LCSH: Environmental health—Juvenile literature. | LCSH: Children and the environment—Juvenile literature.
Classification: LCC RA566.235 .C54 2022 | DDC j333.72—dc23

Library of Congress Control Number: 2021934065

Summary: This illustrated nonfiction book for middle-grade readers explores our right to a healthy environment and introduces the stories of people fighting for change.

Orca Book Publishers is committed to reducing the consumption of nonrenewable resources in the making of our books. We make every effort to use materials that support a sustainable future.

Orca Book Publishers gratefully acknowledges the support for its publishing programs provided by the following agencies: the Government of Canada, the Canada Council for the Arts and the Province of British Columbia through the BC Arts Council and the Book Publishing Tax Credit.

Cover and interior artwork by Julie McLaughlin
Design by Rachel Page
Edited by Kirstie Hudson

Printed and bound in South Korea.

25 24 23 22 • 1 2 3 4

*For Owen and all the children and youth
who stand up for what they believe in.*

Contents

Introduction

When I was in elementary school in Saskatchewan, sometimes the water wasn't safe to drink unless we boiled it first. Now I live in a different part of Canada, and I've never had to boil my water. But I know now that many people in North America still have to boil their water every day. Why? Why, in the same country, do some people have safe water while others don't?

Once, when I was in eighth grade, my friends and I left school for the day and took the bus downtown to attend a protest against a war in Iraq. Millions of barrels of oil had been spilled. Smoke from fire filled the air, choking the people who lived there. Their water was poisoned. It was the first time I'd thought about how much our health is affected by our environment, and how people often don't have a say in how the resources they depend on are cared for.

Later I had the chance to travel to Guyana, South America. I pitched in to help build a well in a community that didn't have a safe source of drinking water. I learned that Guyana had many mines, and at that time, laws weren't strong

In Guyana, the rainforest, rivers and waterfalls, including 741-foot (226-meter) Kaieteur Falls, provide habitat for animals and inspirational places for people to visit.
RICHARD MCMANUS

My son, Owen, and me at the September 27, 2019, climate strike in Vancouver, BC. What will our climate look like for future generations?
MEGAN CLENDENAN

enough to stop polluters from dumping chemicals from those mines into the rivers that people depended on for water to drink and fish to eat. My mom worked for a time at a dry cleaner's, where she was exposed to toxic chemicals. Later she got cancer and passed away. Although I'll never know for sure, I still wonder—how did all those chemicals she breathed at work affect her health?

Everyone, from me to you to people on the other side of the world, depends on clean air to breathe, safe water to drink and nutritious food—and so does every form of life on the planet, from oak trees to grizzly bears to ladybugs. Clean air and fresh water give people a better chance to fight off health threats, such as the COVID-19 virus. But what if your drinking water is dangerous, your air is polluted and your food is contaminated? What if you live in a city that floods as the sea rises? What can you do about that? Do you have the right to demand change? And what about trees, rivers and animals? Do they have rights too? I wanted to learn more about how we can protect both our own health and our environment. That led me to wonder, Do we have the right to a healthy environment? And if we don't, what can we do?

One One Earth to Share

One

IT'S A FACT: NATURE MAKES US HAPPIER AND HEALTHIER

Building a fort, playing in the park or swimming in a lake are not only fun, but they also make you feel better. Just being outside in fresh air can be good for your health. Healthier hearts, less *anxiety* and vitamin D from the sun are some great benefits to being outside. Some doctors are now writing prescriptions for nature! Learning in nature has been shown to help students perform better in school by improving focus, boosting creativity and lowering stress.

Each of our senses can bring out nature's benefits. Have you ever run your hand through the sand or felt the bark of a tree? It feels good, even if we're not sure why. Sometimes when I'm digging in my garden, I take a whiff and notice that the soil actually smells good. It turns out there's a reason for that. *Mycobacterium vaccae* is a type of *bacteria* found in the soil. It's known as the "happy bacteria" because it helps our brains produce more serotonin, a chemical that many

Forest bathing, which is spending time in nature, can reduce stress, depression and anger. Walk in bare feet or dig into the dirt and take in the smell.
GAWRAV SINHA/GETTY IMAGES

Each season offers different things to explore, like these crunchy and colorful autumn leaves.
ARTEM KNIAZ/SHUTTERSTOCK.COM

Megan Clendenan

scientists believe is connected to the feeling of happiness. Besides boosting our mood, happy bacteria can strengthen our immune system and protect us from developing allergies.

AIR + WATER + SOIL = LIFE!

Air!

When the sun comes out, I like to head to the closest green space to enjoy the air. Maybe you like to go to your backyard or a local park or beach. Although we can't see it when we look up, Earth is surrounded by an **atmosphere** that gives us the air we and all other living things need to breathe. There's no doubt that fresh, clean air is good for the body, and it keeps us alive! Fresh air also improves our concentration, mood and energy.

Water!

Although you might not feel it, more than half of your body is made up of water. Water does much more than quench our thirst. It regulates our temperature and keeps our organs—including our brain—healthy. Each person on the planet requires 4.5 to 11 gallons (20 to 50 liters) of clean, safe water a day for drinking, cooking, bathing and washing hands. Clean water can also help with learning. When children have safe water to drink, they are more likely to go to school and concentrate on their lessons and are less likely to get sick.

Soil!

You might have heard the expression "you are what you eat," but how about what your food eats? That's the *soil*—and the soil is worth thinking about. Soil isn't just dirt. It's a mixture of minerals, water and the decaying remains of once-living plants and animals. Good soil is also packed with tiny living

Dip your hands in the water. Touch fallen leaves and slippery rocks. What might you discover if you spend a day watching a stream flow by?
SOLSTOCK/GETTY IMAGES

Community gardens like this one bring people of all ages together to build connections, learn about gardening and access healthy fresh fruits and vegetables.
SOLSTOCK/GETTY IMAGES

One in four ingredients in modern medicines come from rainforest plants. How many more medicines could be discovered in nature?

creatures that help provide nutrients, water and oxygen to growing plants. Soil is where most of the food we eat is grown. Healthy soil grows nutritious food that helps us grow!

PLANTING THE FIRST SEEDS

Humans are one of 8.7 billion forms of life on Earth. That's a lot of life that needs fresh water to drink and clean air to breathe. During the **Paleolithic period**, also known as the Old Stone Age, humans lived in small groups. They gathered wild berries and greens, hunted local animals and caught fish. They ate insects. They didn't produce food, so they moved to find different resources during changing seasons. Although it might have been tempting to eat every last one of the juicy blackberries in late summer, they knew some had to fall to the ground to become the seeds for the following year.

Humans fit into the seasons, along with the animals, the rivers and the trees.

Then, about 12,000 years ago (maybe much earlier!), humans began to plant wild species of plants. This may not sound like a big deal, but it was the beginning of farming. Farming changed everything for humans. Once we learned how to farm, we were able to stay in one place. We built settlements protected by high walls and began to change the land to suit ourselves.

CANNONBALLS TO THE SKY

When farming started, the world population is estimated to have been around five million people. By 2021 our population was almost eight billion. As the population has grown, humans have needed to come up with new ways to collect and store Earth's resources, such as water. Since ancient times people have found many ways to store water, from ponds to tanks to pipes that stretch for hundreds of miles. Humans

In Mongolia, many people still move house with the seasons, herding their animals and taking along their possessions—which in today's world include cell phones and solar panels. RAWPIXEL/GETTY IMAGES

Earth Guardians

Earth Guardians began in 1992 as an alternative high school with 25 students in Hawaii focused on protecting the environment. They restored sandalwood forests and blocked the toxic burning of sugarcane. The program evolved into an organization that trains youth on ways to create change for the environment. More and more people got involved, and today there are thousands of Earth Guardian youth on six continents. Earth Guardian teams across the globe, called crews, help their local communities. They use art, music, protests and even court challenges. They have worked to stop **pesticides** from being sprayed in public parks in North America, offered human rights education to 15,000 women and youth in India and created information on how to fight **climate change** for hundreds of thousands of students in the United States.

have even tried to make it rain during times of **drought**. In the 1800s, some **settlers** in North America thought that firing cannonballs might shake the sky into pouring out rain!

In the last few hundred years, we have moved from storing water to changing the flow of rivers themselves. A dam is a concrete structure built across a river and designed to stop the flow of water. The water is held in a "lake" called a reservoir, then used to water crops on farms, provide drinking water or generate electricity. More than 60,000 large dams have changed the flow of water around the planet. This kind of huge change is positive for some people, but it has also forced many other people to abandon their homes due to flooding and has destroyed the **habitat** of many animals. We are changing the environment in ways that are not always respectful of the things we depend on—clean air, fresh water and healthy soil.

Some Indigenous Peoples of North America, including the Navajo and the Iroquois, grow corn, beans and squash together, a form of companion planting known as the Three Sisters, which keeps the soil healthy and naturally controls pesky pests without chemicals.

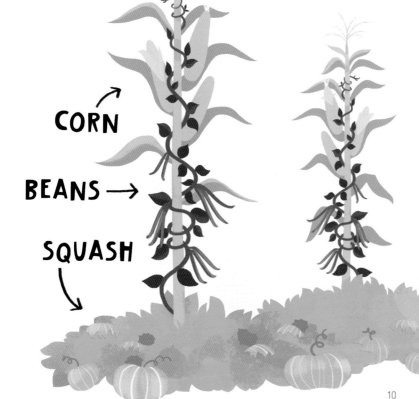

CORN

BEANS →

SQUASH

HOW MANY EARTHS DO WE NEED?

We've always depended on nature for materials, such as wood to build our homes and make paper, and cotton and wool to make our clothes. But beginning in the 1700s the **Industrial Revolution** changed our relationship with nature. It was the process of moving from a world powered by humans, animals, wind and water to one powered more and more by machines. New inventions, such as the steam engine, often fueled by coal, meant people could produce paper and manufacture clothing much faster and in larger quantities. Factories were built, and with them came new problems. Black coal fumes spewed from chimneys into the air. Many factories discharged **toxic** chemical waste directly into nearby rivers and canals, which then seeped into the soil. And for some people, nature became like a never-ending store filled with wood, water and gold.

The Three Gorges Dam in China is the world's largest dam. It has forced more than 1.4 million people to move and flooded two cities, 114 towns and 1,680 villages along the riverbanks.
ISABEL KENDZIOR/SHUTTERSTOCK.COM

11

TOXIC TROUBLES

In the 1800s, the River Thames that flows through London, England, became a dumping ground for human waste, dead rats and toxic materials from nearby factories. Waste transformed the river into a brown, stinky mess. By 1858 London had already had three outbreaks of cholera, an infectious disease caused by contaminated water, which had killed more than 30,000 Londoners. Even though a local doctor named John Snow had proved it was the water that was contaminated, people thought the smell alone could kill them. During the summer of 1858, the smell became so dreadful it was known as the Great Stink. After that, an engineer named Joseph Bazalgette designed a system of brick-lined tunnels to transport all the stinky mess away from central London, saving lives, improving health and helping clear the air.

The Amazon rainforest, which plays an important role in balancing global climate, is under threat by deforestation. As the trees disappear, the forest absorbs less and less carbon dioxide from the atmosphere.
LUOMAN/GETTY IMAGES

Today we still take more than we need to survive—and some people take much more than others. Right now humans are using more resources each year than Earth can sustain over the long term. We do this in many ways, including cutting down too many trees and emitting more **carbon dioxide** than Earth can absorb. By some calculations, humans will need the resources from about 1.7 Earths each year to continue to meet our current demands. But we don't have 1.7 Earths.

WHEN THE AIR IS THICK

My teacher friend Nina once told me a story about school-children in Los Angeles in the 1980s. They colored the moon orange, because that's the only color they'd ever seen it due to all the **pollution** in the air. With more factories, jet planes and cars, we have more pollution. Air pollution creates smog, that brown haze you might have seen hanging over your city.

Smog is a thick mess of smoke and fog. Smog isn't just ugly—it's deadly.

In December 1952, London, England, experienced what is now known as the Great Smog. London was home to many factories that burned coal and created pollution. During the Great Smog, cold air was trapped below the warm air above, a condition called a *temperature inversion*. The pollution stayed close to the ground and could not be released into the sky. For five days the dense smog suffocated London, blackening the sky. People couldn't see, and many got lost trying to find their way home. Thousands of people died during these five days, and up to 12,000 more died afterward from damaged lungs and other illnesses caused by the pollution.

London wasn't the only city choked by smog. In 1960 black rain fell in Boston, a toxic mix of rain, coal and oil.

It's a Fact

We each breathe in about 2,200 to 3,075 gallons (10,000 to 14,000 liters) of air every day.

In the summer of 2020, Los Angeles experienced an extreme heat wave alongside smoke from nearby major wildfires, creating the city's worst air pollution in 26 years.
ROBERT LANDAU/GETTY IMAGES

In 1991, in the mountains of India, black snow fell. It was a mystery for years, until scientists connected the black snow to oil wells on fire in Kuwait, a country more than 2,000 miles (3,300 kilometers) away! Today people in thousands of cities around the world breathe in polluted air and smog.

Polluted air irritates your eyes and throat and damages your lungs and heart. One kind of air pollution, called **particulate matter (PM)**, or particle pollution, can reach deep into your lungs and even get into your bloodstream, causing serious problems. Researchers have found that kids who grow up breathing polluted air are at greater risk of developing such conditions as heart disease and cancer later in life. Pollution can cause asthma and make it harder for their lungs to take in and hold air as they grow into adults.

> The Earth is what we all have in common.
>
> **—WENDELL BERRY,**
> environmental activist
> and author

People in this neighborhood in Shanxi, China, live and work in the shadows of giant smokestacks. Burning coal creates carbon dioxide emissions that are unhealthy for both people and the planet.
KEVIN FRAYER/GETTY IMAGES

When toxic chemicals such as mercury are released from factories into rivers, streams or lakes, they make it unsafe to eat the fish or drink the water from those waterways. SCOTT OLSON/GETTY IMAGES

WE'RE ALL THIRSTY

I live in a community where I can turn on the tap when I'm thirsty and have safe, clean water to drink. Finding a toilet to use is not a problem, and pipes carry waste away to a treatment facility, keeping my family and my community safe from harmful bacteria. But in some parts of Canada, many Indigenous communities don't have access to safe water. When I visited Guyana, I brought a small portable water filter so I could collect water close to the village, but many people who lived in the community I visited had always travelled much farther to find clean water.

In many communities around the world, people can't rely on their drinking water because of pollution caused by *industrial waste*. Each year more people die from unsafe water than from war. Water can also be contaminated by *parasites* that can cause diseases, such as giardia or cryptosporidium,

When water runs dry in a community such as this one in northeastern Brazil, residents have to rely on trucks to deliver water.
JOA_SOUZA/GETTY IMAGES

or harmful bacteria that can cause cholera or typhoid. Cholera can cause severe diarrhea, resulting in dehydration, which means people lose too much fluid from their bodies. This can be dangerous and, in extreme cases, fatal.

In many countries, including Liberia, the Ivory Coast, Peru and Indonesia, millions of people have to walk long distances to collect safe water. Globally, children spend 200 million hours each day collecting water. On average, girls walk 3.7 miles (6 kilometers) a day, carrying 5 gallons (20 liters) of water. Some walk as long as two hours each way. Gathering water can also be dangerous as they risk encountering violence along the way.

Changing weather patterns are also threatening the water supplies for entire cities. In 2014, São Paulo, Brazil, population 22 million, nearly ran out of water. The city reservoirs had less than 5 percent of their capacity. Residents had less than 20 days of water left before the rains finally returned. In 2018, after three years of poor rainfall,

Cape Town, South Africa, was in danger of running out of water and turning off the city taps. The city took drastic action, and the four million residents were restricted to a maximum of 13 gallons (50 liters) of water per day. In contrast, each person in the United States uses an average of 88 gallons (333 liters) of water at home each day. By 2020, the rains returned to fill the Cape Town reservoirs, but the situation could happen again, depending on weather patterns.

HIDDEN AND NOT-SO-HIDDEN POISON

Manufactured chemicals are in all the products we use—furniture, rugs, shampoo, toys, electronics and even our food, soil and water. Scientists have found traces of toxic chemicals everywhere on Earth, even in the most remote places, such as the deep ocean and Antarctica. In 1930, humans produced about 1.1 million tons (1 million metric tons) of chemicals every year. By the year 2019 we were producing about 2.3 billion tons (2.1 billion metric tons) of chemicals.

YOU BE THE JUDGE

When the pipes run dry

Mexico City is one of the world's largest cities. It gets huge amounts of rain for five months of the year, but more than 21 million residents still don't have enough water. Hundreds of miles of pipes bring in water from faraway rivers and lakes. But the water isn't distributed equally. On the east side of the city, the poorer side, some residents can't get a drop of water for days or even months. But on the west side, there's enough water for everyone—even golf courses. If you were the judge, what would you do?

During the 2018 drought in Cape Town, South Africa, people lined up with water jugs to collect natural spring water to drink.
MARK FISHER/SHUTTERSTOCK.COM

Rubber ducks make great bath toys, but many still contain high levels of chemicals, including phthalates.
ROBERT READER/GETTY IMAGES

It's a Fact

In Kenya, where climate change has caused higher temperatures and less predictable rainfall, many people are switching from herding cattle to herding camels. Camels provide nutritious milk and can survive without water for up to two weeks.

That's 2,000 times more chemicals, which is a lot for our water, air and soil—and our bodies—to absorb.

Some chemicals have helped keep us safe. Chemotherapy is a treatment that uses powerful chemicals to treat cancer. During the COVID-19 pandemic, keeping clean to stay safe was on everyone's mind. Disinfectants, which are chemicals that kill dangerous bacteria, mold and viruses on surfaces, help us prevent the spread of illnesses.

But many of the chemicals we use can be harmful to human health and haven't been tested for safety. **Phthalates**, chemicals used to soften plastic, are used in almost everything, including cosmetics, cleaners and food packaging. They were an ingredient in toys for many years. Then scientists found they could be harmful to our health. Although there are still different opinions about how harmful they might be, people protested their use in toys. Eventually, many countries, including the United States and members of the European Union, banned a number of types of phthalates in toys. As we'll see later in the book, when people stand up for their environmental rights, it can make a real difference.

PLANET-SIZED CHANGE

By the 1800s, with the Industrial Revolution well underway, scientists studying Earth's atmosphere found that it acts the same way as a glass greenhouse. Heat and light from the sun enter our atmosphere and are trapped inside. This is called the greenhouse effect. The greenhouse effect allows life on Earth to exist. But while the greenhouse effect keeps our planet livable, there's only so much heat that's needed. Cars, planes and factories burn **fossil fuels** and create **emissions**. These emissions create **greenhouse gases** that trap heat in Earth's atmosphere, making the temperature rise and changing the **climate**.

Earth has cycled in and out of warmer and cooler times in the past. But when temperatures rose, they did so over about 5,000 years. In the past 100 years, Earth's average temperature has climbed by about 1.25 degrees Fahrenheit

In 2010 ash from Iceland's Eyjafjallajökull volcano rose as high as 26,000 feet (8,000 meters), filling the sky with smoke. But volcanic eruptions release less than 1 percent of the carbon dioxide released by human activities in an average year. PAUL SOUDERS/GETTY IMAGES

YOU BE THE JUDGE

Access to clean water

For the people of the Attawapiskat First Nation in northern Ontario, the simple act of having a safe drink of water from the tap has not been possible for decades. Residents have to fill water jugs at one of two watering stations. But people still rely on tap water to take baths and to wash their dishes. In July 2019, tests showed that the town's tap water had high levels of harmful substances. People were warned not to take long showers or use the water to wash their food. But in towns and cities in other parts of the same province, people have regular access to safe, clean water. This is the situation in many small towns and Indigenous communities in North America. Dangerous bacteria, chemicals from mines and paper mills, and pesticides from farms can all make water unsafe to drink. Shouldn't all communities in the same country have access to safe water? If you were the judge, what would you do?

What if your country sank?

Kiribati is a small nation in the south Pacific, made up of 33 small islands. With rising sea levels, Kiribati may be flooded and uninhabitable within the next few decades. Already floods destroy homes and crops and contaminate drinking-water sources with seawater. The country's government is considering buying land in neighboring countries to secure a home for its population. Kiribati is one example of a place where climate change will force people to leave their homes and their country. Should they have the right to move to another country? If you were the judge, what would you do?

(0.7 degrees Celsius). That's 10 times faster than the average rate of warming after an *ice age*.

A difference in temperature of around one degree might not sound like very much, but during the last ice age, when the planet was still partly covered in ice sheets 3,000 feet (914 meters) thick, average temperatures were just 7 to 16 degrees Fahrenheit (5 to 9 degrees Celsius) cooler than they are now. Today, only two ice sheets remain at the North and South Poles. The Antarctic ice sheet alone is as big as the surface area of the United States and Mexico combined. If it melted, the sea level could rise by about 60 meters (200 feet).

When I think about climate change, the first images I have are of disappearing glaciers in Antarctica and polar bears stranded on melting Arctic ice. But it's so much more than that. It includes extreme weather like hurricanes, floods and wildfires. In September 2019, Hurricane Dorian hit the Bahamas, an island nation in the Caribbean. It was the most intense storm the Bahamas had ever experienced. Winds of up to 185 miles (295 kilometers) per hour destroyed most structures. At least 70,000 people were left homeless. In October 2019, England received record amounts of rain. Rivers flooded towns and railway stations, and many people had to evacuate their homes.

In Bangladesh, a country where much of the land is close to the ocean, rising sea levels have caused millions of people to lose their farms. Storms destroy homes, and the salty ocean contaminates fresh water, leaving millions of people without enough to drink. By 2050 rising sea levels may force more than 20 million Bangladeshi people to move to higher ground.

Climate change affects everything, from the places we live to the water we drink to the air we breathe.

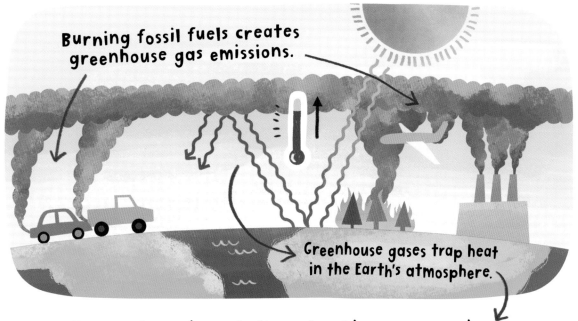

Burning fossil fuels creates greenhouse gas emissions.

Greenhouse gases trap heat in the Earth's atmosphere.

Temperatures rise on both land and in oceans, causing

CLIMATE CHANGE

higher temperatures & heat waves

stronger storms

droughts & desertification

rising sea levels & flooding

wildfires

climate migration

The millions of animals we raise for meat and milk make more than a stink. Methane gas from cows, sheep and goats produces as much as 14.5 percent of global greenhouse gas emissions.
HORACIO SELVA/SHUTTERSTOCK.COM

CLIMATE CHANGE HAS NO BORDERS

Although there are currently 195 individual countries in the world, we all share one planet. When human rights meet climate change, we have **climate justice**. Climate justice recognizes that although many people contribute to climate change, its effects impact some people more than others.

Countries in hot regions near the equator are especially vulnerable to climate change. In 2019 Cyclone Idai devastated Mozambique, one of the poorest nations in the world and with far lower emissions than most other countries. The cyclone flooded huge areas and almost destroyed the entire city of Beira. Thousands of people had to move to temporary camps because they had lost their homes. In Central America, climate change has already changed people's lives. There is now less rain, so farmers can no longer depend on growing coffee, maize and beans to feed their families and earn money to live. It's not just hot places that are affected. In Newtok, Alaska, climate change has caused enough flooding and erosion that the small village has begun to crumble into the sea. In October 2019, Newtok's families started to move to a new village, Mertarvik.

Many people, sometimes called *climate migrants*, are forced to leave their homes due to the effects of climate change, such as lack of water or flooding. The **United Nations** estimates that more than 20 million people each year become climate migrants. Many are children. For example, in the Caribbean, home to many small island nations, a series of severe tropical cyclones and hurricanes forced 3.4 million people, including 761,000 children, to leave their homes in a five-year time period, from 2014 to 2018.

It's a Fact

If everyone on the planet used resources the way people do in both the United States and Canada, a whole year's worth of what Earth can provide would be used up in just 72 days.

Polar bears depend on Arctic ice as a platform for hunting seals, but in the Canadian Arctic, the temperature has increased at a rate that is nearly three times the global average. FLORIDASTOCK/ SHUTTERSTOCK.COM

Wind farms like this one in Guangdong, China, produce electricity from wind, with no need to burn fossil fuels. China is the world's top producer of wind energy.
YUHAN LIAO/GETTY IMAGES

WHAT ARE YOUR RIGHTS?

As we've seen, even though humans depend on this planet's natural resources to live a healthy life, many people now live in an environment that is harmful to their health or cannot provide them with enough nutritious food, clean air or fresh water. At the same time, others have more than they need and emit significant greenhouse gases.

Human rights are freedoms that each human, no matter who they are or where they were born, is entitled to have.

RIGHT TO LIVE

RIGHT to SPeak UP!

EQUALITY = FOR = ALL

They include the right to be free and the right to be treated equally, as well as the right to life itself. When they are upheld, human rights are an important tool for keeping people safe.

Should you be able to eat uncontaminated food, breathe clean air and drink safe water? Should your neighbors, your friends and the people in the next town or on the other side of the planet be able to do the same? Do you have the right to a healthy environment?

Right to Live Free of Discrimination

RIGHT TO LEARN

freedom to Think

Two
Words Have Power

When the elements of survival we all depend on are threatened, people's health, well-being and even their lives are also threatened. Defending human rights and protecting the planet must go hand in hand.

When people talk about the right to a healthy environment, they mean that all humans should have the legal right to breathe clean air, drink clean water and eat uncontaminated food. This is exciting. It could help bring benefits such as equal access to resources and greater protections for all Earth's animals from toxic chemicals and other forms of pollution.

Acknowledging the right to a healthy environment as a human right in a nation's **constitution**, the same as your right to free speech and your right to live free of **discrimination**, is an important step toward protecting both people and the planet. When a right is legally recognized, or protected in writing, it means there are processes citizens can follow if

People take to the streets of New York City in September 2019 to demand action on climate change.
SPENCER PLATT/GETTY IMAGES

27

the right is not being upheld or respected. We will look at all these possibilities later in the book, as well as ways young people are working to ensure their legal rights are upheld.

A RIVER CATCHES FIRE

The idea of caring for and respecting the natural world has been part of many Indigenous cultures for generations. Many take the view that we have both rights and responsibilities to protect land so that it may be kept safe for generations to come. For example, the Mi'kmaq, an Indigenous People of the area we know today as Eastern Canada, recognize that all things in the natural world are interconnected and impose legal obligations on community members to use the resources they need in a *sustainable* way. The Haida Nation off British Columbia's west coast believes that the land must be protected above all else, because it is the foundation for all life. Animals and plants are regarded as equal to or higher than humans, as both play an important role in keeping nature healthy.

Not all cultures have shared this sense of responsibility, and as you read in chapter 1, we are now using more resources, causing more pollution and emitting more greenhouse gasses than our planet can handle.

In the last 70 years, a number of big polluting events have caught people's attention. In the 1950s, people in Los Angeles breathed some of the dirtiest air in the world. Pollution from steel and chemical plants, cars and backyard trash burning stank up the city. Parents kept children out

of school. Emergency rooms were kept busy. People began to make the connection between dirty air and health problems such as asthma and lung cancer.

Also in the 1950s, a strange illness began to circulate in the town of Minamata, Japan. People's legs were going numb, some had difficulty hearing or seeing, and some had brain damage. The cause, it turned out, was mercury poisoning. Mercury had been dumped in a river by a manufacturing factory for years. Eventually fish were poisoned and then so were the people who ate the fish.

In 1967 an oil tanker called the SS *Torrey Canyon* hit a reef off the coast of England. It split open, spewing out 129,000 tons (117,000 metric tons) of oil. Hundreds of miles of coastline were covered in black goo, and thousands of seabirds died. Many people volunteered to come help clean up the mess.

No child should grow up not knowing what clean water is, or never knowing what running water is. We all have a right to this water as we need it—not just rich people, all people.

—AUTUMN PELTIER, speaking to the United Nations General Assembly on World Water Day, March 22, 2018

Autumn Peltier of the Wiikwemkoong Unceded Territory, a First Nation on Manitoulin Island, ON, speaking here at the Global Landscapes Forum in 2019, has been standing up to protect water since she was eight years old.
JUSTIN DAVEY/GLOBAL LANDSCAPES FORUM

Cleaning up after an oil spill is dirty, dangerous work. These workers are helping clean up Ao Prao Beach on Samet Island, Thailand, after a crude-oil spill in 2013.
KAJORNYOT/DREAMSTIME.COM

In June 1969, the Cuyahoga River near Cleveland, Ohio, caught fire. Cleveland was home to many factories that had been dumping garbage, oil and other toxic chemicals into the river. The fire likely began when sparks from a passing train lit up pieces of floating garbage covered in oil. It wasn't the first time the river had caught fire, but this time people took notice. *Time* magazine published an article stating that the river "oozes rather than flows." Nearby Lake Erie, one of the five Great Lakes, was so polluted by toxic chemicals and pesticides dumped by nearby factories that it was declared "dead." In 1970, 20 million people participated in the first Earth Day in the United States. With all these events, the environment was in the news and on many people's minds.

RIGHT TO HEALTHY FOOD & CLEAN WATER

FREEDOM OF EXPRESSION

FREEDOM OF RELIGION

RIGHT TO HEALTH CARE & SUPPORT

greater human rights lead to
GREATER EQUALITY

RIGHT TO ACCESSIBILITY

FREEDOM FROM RACIAL OR GENDER DISCRIMINATION

RIGHT TO EDUCATION

YOU BE THE JUDGE

Why aren't people treated equally?

Today, as well as throughout history, the way people are treated is often determined by the color of their skin, their culture, their gender or whether they are rich or poor. World War II was fought from 1939 to 1945. During the war, six million Jewish people, as well as 11 million others—including people with disabilities, members of the *LGBTQ+* community and the Romani people—were killed because of how they looked, what they believed in and where they came from. After the war, many people felt something needed to be done to protect people. That's why the United Nations was formed. Countries sent representatives to be a part of the United Nations, and together they created a list of rights they believed all humans should have. In 1948 the United Nations agreed on the Universal Declaration of Human Rights. It wasn't perfect, and not every country agreed, but it was a start.

Though the United Nations has helped many nations work together on improving human rights, each country creates its own laws. Unfortunately, millions still face discrimination, unequal treatment and *persecution*. For example, LGBTQ+ people are denied the right to marry in many places, including Russia, India and parts of the United States. People who practice certain religions, such as the Rohingya people, are persecuted for what they believe. Many women are paid less than men for doing the same work. In some places, children must work instead of going to school. And even when human rights are protected by law, those laws aren't always enforced. If you were the judge, what would you do?

ANIMALS LIVE HERE TOO

Rachel Carson loved exploring nature when she was a child. She later published *Silent Spring*, a book that raised awareness of the dangers of chemical pesticides. CARSON FAMILY

In 1963 there were only 417 nesting pairs of bald eagles in the continental United States. After DDT was banned, eagle numbers began to rise. Biologists estimate that there are around 14,000 nesting pairs in the lower 48 states today. MARK NEWMAN/GETTY IMAGES

From pandas and polar bears to beetles and birds, animals are also affected by toxic chemicals in the air, water and land. One scientist, Rachel Carson, helped show how pollution can affect every part of the ecosystem. Carson grew up on a farm, surrounded by nature. She was curious about birds, insects, flowers and all parts of the natural world. She loved writing, and she published her first story in a magazine at age 11. She became a biologist at a time when more and more pesticides were being used on food crops.

In 1962 she wrote a book called *Silent Spring*. It told how DDT, a type of pesticide used to kill insects in farmers' fields and gardens, was poisoning birds, fish and other wildlife. DDT caused the eggshells of birds of prey such as the bald eagle to become so thin that they often broke, and the birds failed to hatch.

Carson's book helped draw attention to the use of chemical pesticides and how it could have negative health consequences we can't foresee, not only for birds, animals and the ecosystem, but also for humans. In 1972 the United States banned DDT use in agriculture. As a result, the bald eagle came back from near extinction in the United States. When we protect our environment, we're also protecting animals and humans—it's a win-win!

Not only are sea otters adorable, but by eating sea urchins they help protect underwater kelp forests. Without otters, sea urchins destroy the kelp forests, which absorb carbon dioxide and provide habitat for fish and mussels.
NEELSKY/SHUTTERSTOCK.COM

NOXIOUS NEIGHBORHOODS

By the 1970s, more people were speaking out about protecting the environment where they lived, worked and played, where they breathed the air and drank the water. People asked questions like, Should some people breathe toxic air so that everyone can have electricity? Whose house should the landfill be built near? Where should all the chemicals be dumped? That's where the idea of *environmental justice*

It's a Fact

In 1943 Los Angeles was choked by brown haze. It was during World War II, so people wondered if it was a chemical attack. It turned out to be smog created by emissions from cars and factories.

Destiny Watford

Destiny Watford was a 17-year-old high school student in 2014 when she learned of a plan to build a trash-burning incinerator in her community of Curtis Bay, near the city of Baltimore. Destiny's family and friends all suffered from health problems such as asthma and lung cancer, caused by emissions from the many factories that were already located in Curtis Bay. The proposed incinerator was to burn 4,000 pounds (1,815 kilograms) of garbage each day and emit 1,240 pounds (563 kilograms) of toxic lead and mercury each year. It was going to be built only 1 mile (1.4 kilometers) from two schools.

Destiny co-founded Free Your Voice to fight for her community's rights. The group organized protests and wrote to their local government. They discovered that the school system, along with other local organizations, planned to buy energy from the incinerator. Destiny's group gave a presentation to their school board to show how much pollution the incinerator would bring and how that would cause even more health problems for their community. Thanks to Destiny's and Free Your Voice's work, the school board, as well as the 22 other customers who had signed a contract with the incinerator, decided to cancel! With no customers to serve, the incinerator was not built. Free Your Voice then brought attention to healthier ideas for their community, such as a solar farm, a recycling depot and more composting facilities.

came from—the understanding that defending human rights and protecting the environment are connected.

Imagine you live in a house that has poisonous lead in the garden soil, or that your air contains toxic particulates because of a nearby factory. Each causes health problems that might affect you for your whole life. So why doesn't your family just move somewhere else? Often it's not that simple. There might not be anywhere else with a job for your parents or a home that they can afford to live in. They may need to stay and take care of your grandparents. There are many reasons why people can't leave their homes, their cities or their countries. I know I wouldn't want to leave my community and all my friends.

In 1979 the state of North Carolina decided to move soil filled with toxic chemicals to a landfill located in Warren County, home to many Black Americans. People asked questions. Why that community? Why not the community down the street? Citizens protested, but they were not listened to. In 1982 truckloads of toxic soil began to arrive. Once again people protested, and many were arrested.

The protesters were not successful in stopping the toxic soil from being brought to the landfill. But they did bring attention to the idea of *environmental racism*. With this type of discrimination, neighborhoods populated mostly by people with low incomes or people of visible minorities, such as Indigenous people or People of Color, are burdened with more environmental hazards than other communities are. Toxic-waste facilities, garbage dumps, pulp mills, factories and other polluting businesses are too often built in these communities. In a study spanning 20 years, researchers discovered that more than half of the people who lived within 1.86 miles (3 kilometers) of toxic-waste facilities in the United States were People of Color.

US Representative Alexandria Ocasio-Cortez speaks to promote the proposed Green New Deal, which is legislation to reduce fossil fuels and create new jobs in clean-energy industries.
CHIP SOMODEVILLA/GETTY IMAGES

You'll remember that environmental justice means treating people fairly with respect to environmental laws and regulations. It means that everyone should be protected from pollution, no matter the color of their skin, their culture, the amount of money they have or their gender. It also means that everybody should have equal access to the benefits nature provides. Not just safe water, clean air and healthy food, but also the joy of running through the grass or sitting quietly next to a towering tree.

ENVIRONMENTAL LAWS

One way to protect human and environmental health is to pass environmental laws. The laws of a country set out the rules. Imagine trying to play a game without everyone knowing the rules! It would be difficult. Laws must be able to be enforced and upheld. Starting in the 1950s, countries began to develop and pass more environmental laws. Laws set limits on air pollution, such as from cars and furnaces, and this helped reduce toxic emissions in the air we breathe. Similar laws were written to limit the release of chemicals into rivers, lakes and other bodies of water. Other laws required companies to get permits before building factories or taking resources such as minerals or trees.

Researchers believe these new laws have meant that millions more people are healthier and have spent less time in hospital. That's a big difference! But in a **democracy**, the people running the country often change every few years. Some politicians believe in environmental protections more than others do, and there is a danger that when someone new takes charge, they will weaken or take away environmental laws. And as we've seen, some people are unfairly exposed to more pollution than others, even with environmental laws in place.

Here are a few of the many environmental laws from around the world:

- Clean Air Act, England, 1956
- Basic Law for Environmental Pollution Control, Japan, 1967
- Clean Air Act, United States, 1970
- Environment (Protection) Act, India, 1986
- Environmental Protection Act, Canada, 1988
- Air Quality Act, South Africa, 2004

HIGHEST LAW OF THE LAND

Human rights are most often written, meaning legally recognized, in a country's constitution. A constitution is a written set of laws containing the rules that guide how a country

YOU BE THE JUDGE

When should polluters be stopped?

Boat Harbour, NS, is home to the Pictou Landing First Nation. It's also where a paper mill dumped chemicals for 53 years. For years people there suffered from health problems, including the third-highest rate of cancer of any Canadian community. They asked for change for decades. They took the government to court. They peacefully protested. It was not until January 31, 2020, that the pulp mill was finally shut down. Should the company have been allowed to pollute one community for 53 years? If you were the judge, what would you do?

Environmental activists in Yogyakarta, Indonesia, peacefully protest to ask their government leaders to act on the climate crisis. PARAMARTA BARI/SHUTTERSTOCK.COM

.

.

It's a Fact

Clean hands require soap and water. During the COVID-19 pandemic, access to water to wash hands was not available for almost three billion people worldwide.

Children in Portugal can breathe easy, thanks to the right to healthy environment.
MAJONIT/SHUTTERSTOCK.COM

works, including what powers the government has and what rights citizens have. The constitution also represents the **values** a country holds. A constitution acts as the highest law of the country. You can think of a constitution as the ultimate rule book. Breaking those rules is a big deal.

Rights written in the constitution are said to be "protected" and are much more difficult to change than ordinary laws. For example, to amend the constitution of the United States, two-thirds of the members of both the House of Representatives and the Senate must vote to approve the change, as well as at least 38 out of 50 states. To change the Canadian Charter of Rights and Freedoms, the House of Commons, the Senate and two-thirds of the provinces representing over 50 percent of Canadians must approve.

Adding the right to live in a healthy environment to the constitution will result in stronger environmental laws because governments must consider what's in the

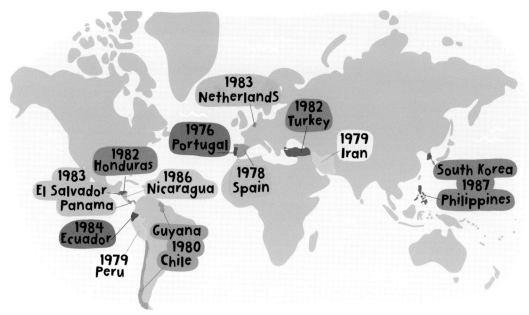

The First 15 Countries to Include the Constitutional Right to Live in a Healthy Environment

constitution when developing all other laws. That's the power of the constitution!

RIGHTS TO THE RESCUE

In 1976 Portugal was the first country to add the right to live in a healthy environment to its constitution. Since then there have been positive benefits for Portugal's citizens. Today almost 99 percent of drinking water in Portugal is free of chemicals. The right was put to the test when a company wanted to build a gas station that would threaten the air quality near an elementary school. A Portuguese court ruled that the gas station would violate the schoolchildren's right to a healthy environment and could not be built. Portugal also guarantees people's right to participate in decision making, encourages citizens to form environmental groups and allows them to go to court if they feel that's what's needed. The right to a healthy environment can be upheld in Portugal because of all these things working together.

Our culture is born of respect, and intimacy with the land and sea and the air around us. Like the forests, the roots of our people are intertwined such that the greatest troubles cannot overcome us. We owe our existence to Haida Gwaii. The living generation accepts the responsibility to ensure that our heritage is passed on to following generations.

–HAIDA NATION
CONSTITUTION

Sharing space to save tigers

India is home to more than 70 percent of the world's tiger population. Tigers are endangered, and reserves have been created to protect tiger habitat. But in the process, Indigenous people have been evicted from their homes. In the Biligiri Rangaswamy Temple Tiger Reserve, the Soligas, a local Indigenous group, have traditionally shared the forest with the tigers. In 2011 the Soligas became the first Indigenous group in India to win the right to stay and live on their traditional lands within a tiger reserve. Since then the number of tigers in their area has nearly doubled, increasing from 35 to 68. There are other Indigenous groups in India that want to return to their traditional lands, also within protected tiger areas. If you were the judge, what would you do?

As of 2019, at least 100 countries have followed Portugal's example and added the right to live in a healthy environment to their constitutions. As well, many other countries have included some form of legal protection, in other types of laws or international agreements, for the right to a healthy environment. In total, close to 200 countries support people's right to live in a healthy environment.

Clean, safe, wholesome, protected and pleasant. These are some of the words countries use to define what they mean by a healthy environment. Many use the phrase "not harmful to health," and others focus on "ecologically balanced." Ecuador even recognizes the rights of future generations, as well as today's citizens.

In Finland, the presence of the right to a healthy environment in the constitution helped stop construction of a dam on the Kemijoki River. Environmental groups went to the **Supreme Court** twice. They argued that the dam would flood 155 square miles (401 square kilometers) of land and affect many people and animals. In January 2020, a court in France cited the right to live in a healthy environment to stop French companies from sending illegal pesticides to other countries. The decision helps keep crops safer and food healthier.

Upholding the right to a healthy environment requires strong environmental laws and processes. Once in place, those laws can lead to positive benefits such as cleaner air, safer drinking water and firmer limits on pollution. They can also increase fairness by protecting land and resources for future generations. When a country recognizes the right to live in a healthy environment in its constitution, it signals that protecting human health and the health of its air, water and land is an important shared value. It's a good first step in making change.

The youth of Grassy Narrows

More than 50 years ago, a pulp mill dumped an estimated 22,000 pounds (9,979 kilograms) of mercury into the Wabigoon River system in northwestern Ontario, poisoning all the plants, fish and animals in more than 155 miles (250 kilometers) of nearby waterways. The pollution continued for decades, and the government has never forced the polluter to clean up. The Asubpeeschoseewagong First Nation (also known as the Grassy Narrows First Nation) lives downstream from where the mercury was dumped. The fish they depend on for food have been poisoned for decades, but many people still eat the fish because it is their only option. For generations, many community members had made a living fishing, but after the mercury poisoning they could no longer do that. Mercury poisoning has caused numerous health problems. Many people suffer from hearing and speech problems and even kidney and brain damage. Mercury can be passed from moms to babies long after the chemical spill happens.

In 2008 youth from Grassy Narrows First Nation walked 1,150 miles (1,851 kilometers) to Toronto to protest the mercury **contamination**. They repeated the journey in 2009 and 2012, and in 2019 more than 40 members of the Grassy Narrows community traveled to Toronto to hold the government accountable for the long-standing environmental contamination, and to demand that the government keep its promise to build a care center for survivors of mercury poisoning. But without a constitutional right to a healthy environment, they are still fighting today.

SHELBY GILSON/PULITZER CENTER

TOXIC TROUBLES

In 1978 Lois Gibbs, a resident of the Love Canal neighborhood in Niagara Falls, NY, was worried because her son kept coming home sick from kindergarten. Many other people were getting sick too. Horrible smells wafted through backyards, and gardens stopped growing. The soles of people's shoes began to disintegrate. Something was very wrong. Lois led her neighbors in a protest and discovered the toxic truth. Their homes and school had been built next to 20,000 pounds (9,072 kilograms) of chemical waste that had been covered with clay. No one had been informed. Everyone marched through the streets, even in the chill of winter. Thousands of residents wrote letters to then president Jimmy Carter. Finally, in 1980, families were offered other homes, away from the pollution.

What if one day a bulldozer showed up to clear your neighborhood forest to build a new parking lot? When we can ask questions, find out more information, talk to other people who might be affected and go to court when needed, these processes help us stand up for our right to live in a healthy environment.

LEFT OUT: WHEN RIGHTS AREN'T PROTECTED

As we've seen, many countries have now protected their citizens' right to a healthy environment in their constitutions. But many countries, including the United States, Canada and Australia, currently do not have the right to live in a healthy environment in their constitutions. When that's the case, citizens have to rely on other rights to try to protect their health and their environment.

The right to life is one of the basic human rights protected by the United Nations Declaration of Human Rights. In places where the right to a healthy environment isn't protected, groups of children and youth have had to go to court to try to force their governments to take serious action to combat climate change and reduce pollution to protect the air, water and soil directly connected to their right to life.

WE'RE NOT DONE FIGHTING

Simply recognizing rights isn't enough—rights need to be upheld with strong, enforceable laws. But those laws also need to be applied equally to everyone in a country. Unfortunately, that's not always the case. Many battles to bring equal rights to people are ongoing. For example, in Canada many Indigenous communities still don't have safe drinking water in their communities. Citizens—including youth and children—are heading to courts around the world to tell their governments that they must enforce the law to safeguard their rights.

STOP!

Attend a meeting. Listen. Give your opinion.

Ask for information. Learn about the laws.

Stand up for the trees and your right to breathe clean air.

Three
All Rise!

SO WHAT'S THE PROBLEM NOW?

The idea that people have the right to live in a healthy environment has been recognized and is supported in some way in close to 200 countries. Now that so many countries have done so, we should be seeing progress in such areas as reducing pollution and slowing climate change. And in some cases, there is positive change. But the fact is, overall pollution is still increasing, resources are being used faster than the planet can handle, and climate change continues. So what's the problem? Why aren't we making better progress?

In 2019 the United Nations released a report on its investigation to figure out this mystery. It discovered that even though there are many more environmental laws in place, the laws on paper aren't always enforced.

Have you ever decided you would keep your room clean all the time, then found that sometimes you were too tired and other times you forgot? Even when we have the best of intentions, changes can be hard to make, and not everything

When laws aren't working to limit pollution, such as that from coal-fired power stations like this one, people can head to court to demand action.
LUKAS SCHULZE/GETTY IMAGES

It's a Fact

When you add up the laws from all countries on Earth, there were 38 times more environmental laws written in 2019 than in 1972.

An Indigenous community member leads a march in support of the Dakota Access Pipeline protesters in November 2016 in Toronto.
ARINDAMBANERJEE/SHUTTERSTOCK.COM

gets done. It's the same for countries. Even in places that have strong environmental laws, enforcing them can be difficult.

Governments don't always have enough money or resources, such as inspectors, to enforce environmental laws. Other times, governments make decisions that are focused on something else, like creating new jobs. And in some places, laws aren't enforced in a way that treats all citizens equally. If environmental laws are not enforced, then the human right to live in a healthy environment is not supported.

KEEPING THINGS FAIR

Environmental justice means that all people, no matter who they are, have the right to be heard and to stand up for themselves and their families. When citizens believe their government is not upholding their rights, they can turn to

STAND UP FOR THE CONSTITUTIONAL RIGHT TO A LIVABLE PLANET

PROTECT Youth & FUTURE GENERATIONS

#LetTheYouthBeHeard

#LeadOnClimate

the courts for help. Courts can decide whether laws are being obeyed and rights are being respected. In many countries, courts have the power to strike down laws that violate the constitution.

The courts have been a place where other groups fighting for equality have found some success, including the **civil rights movement.** Like groups in the civil rights movement, people fighting for environmental rights believe in equal protection for all people, and that no one group should have to experience more pollution than any other group.

Around the world, courts have heard from citizens who believe in their right to live in a healthy environment. Court decisions based on the right to a healthy environment have been made in more than 50 nations. Many people—including children and youth—are heading to court to fight legal battles on issues from pollution to climate change.

Protesters rally in October 2018 outside the US Supreme Court in Washington, DC, in support of the *Juliana v. United States* climate justice lawsuit.
WIN MCNAMEE/GETTY IMAGES

COURT FIGHTS FOR RIGHTS

Mahesh Chander Mehta

Case file: A busy lawyer helps India push back on polluters

The Supreme Court of India was one of the first courts to protect citizen rights to a clean and healthy environment. One environmental lawyer, Mahesh Chander Mehta, has won more than 40 environmental cases in India—this might be a world record for an environmental lawyer!

In 1985 the Ganges River, which millions of people depend on for water, caught fire because so much industrial pollution had been dumped in the river. Mehta went to the Supreme Court of India, and as a result 5,000 factories along the river had to install pollution-control devices and 300 factories were closed. In New Delhi, the capital of India, another of Mehta's Supreme Court cases resulted in an order that 9,000 polluting factories be relocated outside the city limits. Mehta brought so many environmental cases to court that at one point a special courtroom was reserved for him every Friday.

Case File: Protecting trees as though they are family

Terri-Lynn Williams-Davidson

In 2004 Haida Nation citizen and lawyer Terri-Lynn Williams-Davidson was part of a legal team that went to the Supreme Court of Canada and successfully halted clear-cut logging in a forest on Haida Gwaii, the island home of the Haida Nation. While the team presented clear scientific evidence of the damage the logging was doing to the forests, it also argued that old-growth red cedar forest is so important to Haida people that the cedar tree is considered an older sister.

Case file: Fighting for the future in the Philippines

The Philippines is a country in the western Pacific Ocean that's made up of more than 7,000 islands. Its rainforests provide food and water to many species, regulate the temperature and clean carbon dioxide from the air. In 1900 there were 53 million acres (21 million hectares) of rainforest, but over time many trees were cut down. In 1987 the Philippines created a new constitution that included the right to a healthy environment. But that didn't stop people from cutting down trees, and by 1988 only 4 percent of the original forest remained. Fifty-one million acres (20.6 million hectares) of forest had been cut down, which is an area about the size of Kansas. As well, the government continued to give logging companies permission to cut down more trees.

Led by environmental lawyer Antonio Oposa Jr., a group of 43 children, which included Oposa's children and those of close friends and family members, decided to go to

Protecting forests means that future generations of children will benefit from cleaner air and water, as well as the opportunity to enjoy climbing trees, just like this boy on Coron Island, Palawan, the Philippines.
PHUONG D. NGUYEN/SHUTTERSTOCK.COM

Antonio Oposa Jr.

court to save what was left of the rainforest before it was too late. They wanted to stop the removal of the remaining old-growth forest because it violated their right to a healthy environment. The Supreme Court of the Philippines ruled in favor of the children! It said the government had a responsibility to respect the environmental rights of children, both today and in the future.

Case file: Botswana—every human needs water to live

The Kalahari San have always lived in harmony with their environment, hunting animals and gathering berries and nuts, but taking only what they need.
WERNER GOETZ/SHUTTERSTOCK.COM

The Kalahari San are an Indigenous people of Botswana, Africa. They live in a dry region with very few sources of water. Their own government blocked them from accessing water on their traditional lands, which are now in an area protected for animals and tourists. The Kalahari, including elderly people and children, had to travel 300 miles (483 kilometers) round trip to access water.

The Kalahari San took their government to the Botswana High Court and argued they were being denied their human right to water. In 2011 the court agreed with the Kalahari San. While this is good news, Botswana does not have the right to a healthy environment protected in its constitution. The Kalahari San are still fighting their government for fair and equal treatment, including access to their land and water.

Shipbreaking is dangerous work, exposing workers and their families to poisonous gases and hazardous chemicals. At least 10 percent of all shipbreaking workers are under the age of 18.
SALVACAMPILLO/SHUTTERSTOCK.COM

Case file: A Bangladeshi lawyer makes a polluter pay

All over the world, huge steel ships carrying everything from cars to crayons motor across oceans. When they become old, their steel is still valuable, but they need to be taken apart. And taking apart ships is a dirty and dangerous job.

Bangladesh is located between India and Myanmar. Chittagong is a coastal city with more than 8.6 million residents and a huge number of people from other parts of the country seeking work. This is one place where the world's big ships go to be broken up. Thousands of workers, some as young as 14, face dangerous working conditions and breathe

Syeda Rizwana Hasan

in chemicals from the ships. These chemicals also leak onto beaches and into the water. Workers and their families, as well as people who live nearby, are exposed to significant pollution.

Beginning in 2003, Syeda Rizwana Hasan, an environmental lawyer from Bangladesh, began to fight in the Supreme Court on behalf of the workers. She wanted to prevent ships from entering Bangladesh unless they were free of toxic substances. She also wanted to stop shipbreaking activities unless workers and the environment were better protected. Her efforts led to the first case in the country's history of a polluter having to pay for breaking the law. By 2009 the Supreme Court had made much stronger rules for the shipbreaking industry. This helped protect the river, the workers and the many people and animals who live in the area.

Case file: Kraków's community rises up against coal smoke

The ancient city of Kraków, Poland, is filled with beautiful medieval castles and soaring churches, set in a valley between mountains. Kraków winters are chilly, and the temperature often sinks below freezing. People burn coal and wood for heat. While having a cozy fire to stay warm doesn't sound terrible, both wood and coal release toxic fumes into the air. Kraków's location means smoke from people's homes doesn't drift away with the wind. Instead it settles on the city and is dangerous for the lungs and hearts of residents.

The pollution got so bad that many children weren't allowed to play outside. Even staying inside, children in Kraków were almost three times more likely to develop asthma than children breathing clean air in other places. Parents lined up to enroll their children in an anti-smog preschool—a school fortified to keep out the dangerous air.

The medieval St. Mary's Church soars above Kraków's Market Square under blue July skies. But in the winter months, the skies turn dark with lung-choking smog from coal and wood fires.
VENTURA CARMONA/GETTY IMAGES

Public-awareness posters like this one are helping the Kraków Smog Alarm start a citywide discussion about air quality, to demand change.
KRAKÓW SMOG ALARM

YOU BE THE JUDGE

Pollution near schools

Children who go to school near busy roads are more likely to have breathing difficulties and develop asthma. An organization in England called Clean Air in London found that 1,148 schools in London were located near busy roads. How do you balance the children's right to breathe clean air with people's desire to drive their cars? If you were the judge, what would you do?

People in Kraków, sick of breathing dirty air, decided to fight back. They believed they had a right to clean air in their own homes. A group of activists known as the Kraków Smog Alarm began fighting for new laws, demanding a ban on home coal furnaces and chimneys with no filters. After years of protests, in 2016 the government banned burning coal and wood in homes. The new ban was fought in court, but in the end the environmental activists won, and a court order upheld the new law.

Case file: A small community from Argentina makes big things happen

The Matanza-Riachuelo river basin near Buenos Aires, Argentina, has been called one of the most polluted places on the planet. For more than 200 years, people in communities along the river have had to live with pollution from chemical factories and toxic pesticides from farms. In some communities, children suffered from lead poisoning, which can cause health problems that stick with them for their whole lives.

By 2004 one small community along the river had had enough. Seventeen people filed a lawsuit against the

Argentinian government, the city of Buenos Aires and 44 businesses. They believed the pollution in the river was violating their right to a healthy environment, which was protected in the constitution of Argentina.

In 2008 the Supreme Court of Argentina decided in favor of the residents. The court said that, based on the right to a healthy environment, the government needed to clean up the river to help people living nearby have a better quality of life. Families near the worst pollution were moved to cleaner homes. Huge amounts of waste were removed from the river. It's still not perfect, but it's a start.

When she was seven years old, Rabab Ali was worried about the future. With the help of her father, an environmental lawyer, she filed a lawsuit on behalf of all Pakistani people in the Supreme Court of Pakistan. QAZI ALI ATHAR

Case file: Taking the government to court over climate change

In 2015 something big happened in the Netherlands. Eight hundred and eighty-six citizens, including many children, took their government to court to protect their right to a healthy environment. As almost a third of the Netherlands is below sea level, the country is especially vulnerable to rising sea levels and flooding—consequences of climate change. People believed that the air and water pollution caused by greenhouse gas emissions threatened the health of both current and future generations. The case was fought in the courts for many years.

On December 20, 2019, the Supreme Court of the Netherlands ruled that the government had violated people's human rights and must act to reduce greenhouse gas emissions by at least 25 percent compared to levels in 1990. It was the first time ever that a court's decision was based on the connection between human rights and climate change. It was also the first time a government was held responsible for its role in climate change. The government has developed an impressive plan to reduce emissions, including investing

It's a Fact

One large tree provides enough oxygen for four people to breathe for one day.

The Urgenda Foundation's climate-case victory in the Dutch Supreme Court sent a message to governments everywhere: It's time to act now, or we will see you in court!
URGENDA FOUNDATION

in solar power, planting more trees, recycling more plastic, enforcing environmental laws and shutting down a coal-fired power plant. This case inspired similar ones in New Zealand, Belgium, Ireland, England and Switzerland.

Case file: Portuguese children fight fires in the court

Many people around the world have had to run from their homes, leaving everything behind, because of wildfires. In California alone, millions of people live in areas where it's so dry because of low rainfall that dangerous fires happen frequently. Many scientists believe these fires are becoming larger and happening more often because of climate change. Hotter temperatures lead to drier vegetation, which sparks more fire.

Firefighters battle a wildfire near Pedrógão Grande in the Leiria region of Portugal in summer 2017.
PABLO BLAZQUEZ DOMINGUEZ/GETTY IMAGES

Canadian youth head to court

Fifteen Canadian youth between the ages of 10 and 19 filed a lawsuit against the government in the Federal Court of Canada in October 2019. They believe the Canadian government is both contributing to and allowing dangerous levels of greenhouse gas emissions. The youth argue that climate change violates their right to life, liberty, security of the person and equal protection under the Canadian Charter of Rights and Freedoms. In November 2020, after a Federal Court judge ruled that they must take their request to a higher court, the youth filed with the Federal Court of Appeal and will not give up on what they believe in.

In the summer of 2017 there was a heat wave in Portugal. The temperatures rose to over 104 degrees Fahrenheit (40 degrees Celsius) in some areas. In one night 60 forest fires started. Even with 1,700 firefighters battling to stop them, fires in the Leiria region killed many people and injured others.

A group of children from Leiria, aged between 5 and 14, decided they needed to act for their future. They believe the wildfires threaten their right to life. They have filed the first climate-change case at the European Court of Human Rights, demanding that 33 countries decrease their greenhouse gas emissions. In a positive development, in November 2020 the court decided that the case will proceed to the next stage, so each of the 33 defendant countries must respond to the complaint. The fact is, borders between countries can't stop fires, extreme weather or pollution. In many cases the big question is, Who's responsible?

I'm taking action on climate change because I have to. I can't live my life as normal when nothing about our climate is normal. I feel the effects of climate change every day, yet in comparison to the rest of the world I have it good. For me, fighting for climate change is about fighting for human rights.

—CECILIA, 15, from Toronto, one of the youth involved in the case

TAKING A CASE TO COURT

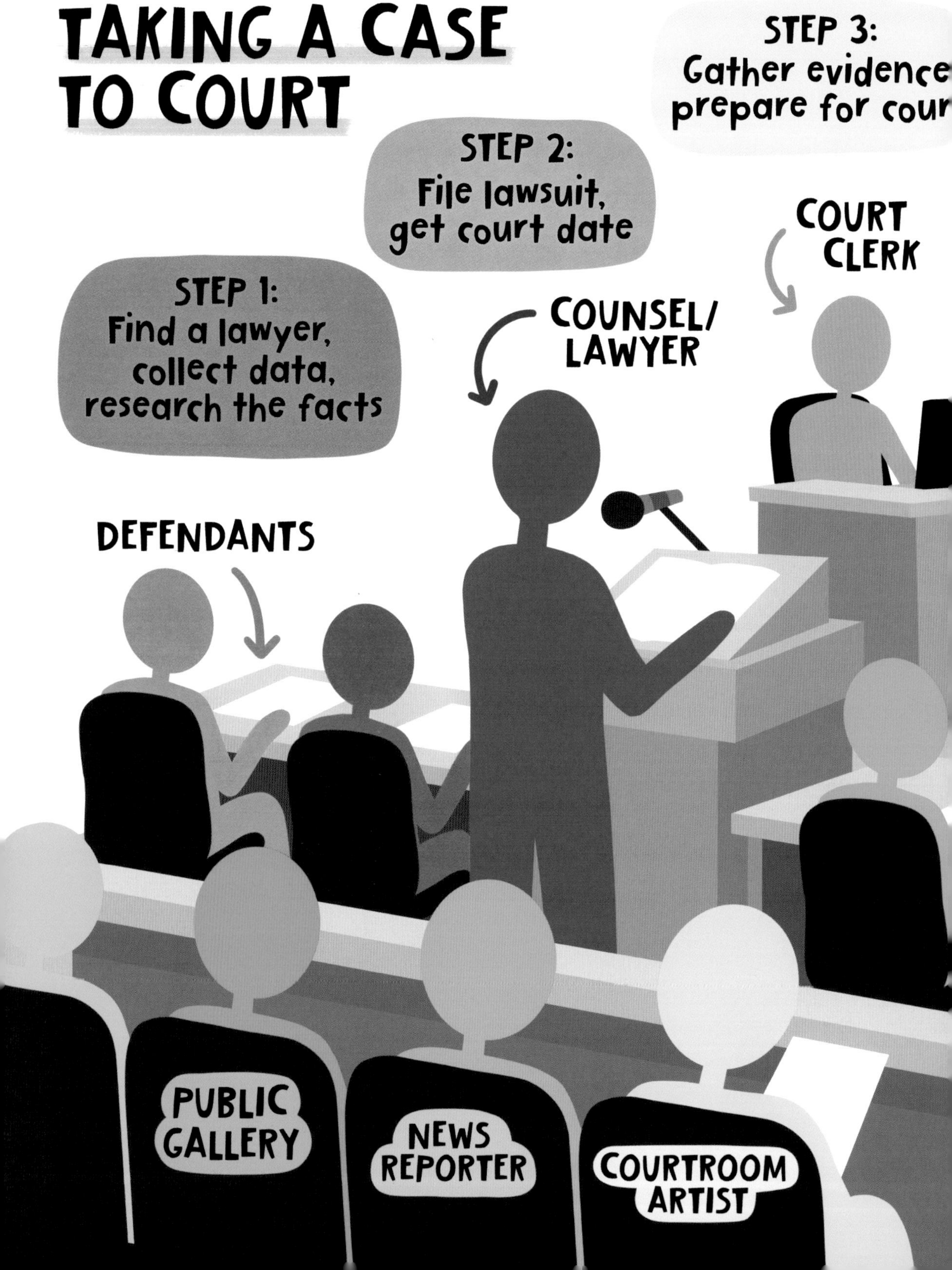

STEP 4:
Day in court!
Present evidence
and arguments

STEP 5:
Wait for judge's decision

AUDIOVISUAL
EQUIPMENT

DESTRUCTION
BY STORM

JUDGE

COURT
REPORTER

WITNESS

PLAINTIFFS

TOXIC TROUBLES

In the 1970s, the trees in the Black Forest in Germany became so damaged that they looked like blackened skeletons. The cause was *acid rain*, which is a form of air pollution. It happens when you burn fossil fuels and they combine with the oxygen and water in the air to become acidic rain or snow. People exposed to acid rain can develop health problems such as asthma and lung cancer. Acid rain is not stopped by any border, so one country's pollution is another country's acid rain. A big question that people asked was, Does a polluter who spreads toxic chemicals into another country have to clean up their mess or can they just walk away? The good news is that in 1979 a number of European countries signed an agreement called the Convention on Long-Range Transboundary Air Pollution. It was a promise to decrease air pollution, and over time it did help reduce acid rain.

GETTING EIGHT BILLION PEOPLE TO COOPERATE ISN'T EASY

At the same time that individual countries were beginning to include the right to live in a healthy environment in their constitutions, countries were meeting to discuss how they could cooperate to fight climate change.

In 1972 in Stockholm, Sweden, the United Nations held the first meeting ever about environmental issues. Representatives from 114 countries attended, as well as scientists and environmental groups. Delegates discussed how to cooperate to protect the environment. Twenty years later, the 1992 Earth Summit (United Nations Conference on Environment and Development) was held in Brazil. The Rio Summit, as it was known, was the biggest meeting to date about people and the environment. Delegates from 178 countries attended, as well as thousands of people representing environmental and social change organizations. Countries signed five international agreements to help protect animals, people and our planet. Three of the agreements were about using natural resources in a sustainable manner, which means using them in a way that will leave enough for people in the future to have their needs met. The other two agreements focused on protecting **biodiversity** and combating climate change. Although the meeting was a step forward for environmental rights, many countries didn't keep their promises. Some countries signed a follow-up agreement in Kyoto, Japan, a few years later, but it wasn't enough to stop climate change.

Then, in 2015, Paris, France hosted an international meeting where countries discussed a new agreement to fight climate change. It is known as the Paris Agreement, and

its main goal is to keep the global temperature rise to well below 3.6 degrees Fahrenheit (2 degrees Celsius). Countries are planning to lower their emissions through such actions as increasing solar or wind power and reducing the use of coal and gas. There is hope that this will make a difference, but no one knows yet how effective the agreement will be. As of January 2021, 190 countries have ratified (formally committed to) the agreement.

The United Nations hopes to one day recognize a global right to a safe, clean, healthy and sustainable environment. This would help pressure countries that do not yet recognize the right to a healthy environment, as well as support those countries that already recognize the right.

Students represent their countries at a Model United Nations conference, which takes place in various countries each year to give participants the chance to gain skills in how to debate, negotiate and compromise.
AMUZUJOE/WIKIMEDIA COMMONS/
CC BY-SA 4.0

If you don't know how to fix it, please stop breaking it!

-SEVERN CULLIS-SUZUKI
at age 12, speaking about environmental problems at the United Nations Conference on Environment and Development, Rio de Janeiro, Brazil, June 11, 1992

Ecuador is one of the most biodiverse places on Earth, with geography that includes mountains, rainforest and the Galápagos Islands. It was the first country to place the rights of nature in its constitution.
AMMIT JACK/SHUTTERSTOCK.COM

YOU BE THE JUDGE

Who should control water?

The Mekong River is the world's twelfth-longest river. It runs through China, Myanmar, Laos, Thailand, Cambodia and Vietnam. There are many dams already on the Mekong, including several in China, which is located upstream of all the other countries. If one country decides to build dams upriver, it affects millions of people who depend on its water farther downstream. Should one country be able to control the flow of the river? If you were the judge, what would you do?

NATURE HAS ITS OWN RIGHTS

We've talked a lot about human rights and how all people should be able to live in a healthy environment. But what about nature? One of the problems with trying to protect the environment by going to court is that nature does not have the same rights as people do. To help solve that problem, some places are giving nature its own legal rights. This is what happened for the Amazon rainforest in Colombia in 2018, when youth took their government to court for not protecting it. And in 2017, New Zealand passed a law recognizing the Whanganui River, the third-longest in the country, as a legal person with rights and responsibilities. The river is no longer owned by humans. It's owned by itself, but it is represented by the Maori people, who can protect the river in court if need be.

A court in India in 2017 gave the Ganges and Yamuna Rivers the same legal protection as a person. Ecuador's 2008 constitution protects the natural world, and anyone can go to court on behalf of nature. In 2011 an Ecuadorian court ruled that a proposed road would violate the Vilcabamba River's right to health, as construction would dump huge amounts of rock, sand and gravel into the river, causing it to flood and affect people who lived nearby. Road construction was halted. Giving nature its own rights is another way to help protect people.

JULIANA V. UNITED STATES

In 2015 a group of youth in the United States sued their federal government for not doing enough to prevent climage change. The first youth to join the case was Kelsey Juliana, who was 19 years old at the time. Kelsey and her family had always been involved in environmental issues. Wildfires in her home state of Oregon were a reminder that climate change was already happening. Twenty youth from 10 different states joined the lawsuit. The youngest was eight years old when

Kelsey Juliana speaks at the 2018 WIRED25 conference in San Francisco with two other *Juliana v. United States* plaintiffs to help bring awareness to why they are fighting for their future. PHILLIP FARAONE/ GETTY IMAGES FOR WIRED

How many factories?

Near Sarnia, ON, the Aamjiwnaang First Nation is located next to more than 35 oil and gas factories. The area is called Chemical Valley. Members of the community are constantly breathing in toxic fumes. Children often can't play outside due to shelter-in-place alarms about fumes. Health problems, especially difficulty with breathing, happen at higher-than-average rates. Creeks where people used to swim now have warning signs, as the chemicals are everywhere. When a company decided it wanted to build yet another factory in Chemical Valley, the community joined together to say, "No more." How many factories should one community have to live next to? If you were the judge, what would you do?

It's a Fact

Earth's richest 10 percent of people produce 50 percent of all fossil fuel emissions.

the case began. Some had experienced major flooding, others rising sea levels. They all believed that climate change would play a big role in the lives of their whole generation. The case argued that their rights to life and liberty are threatened because their government continues to build big developments, such as pipelines and oil refineries, that add to climate change.

For years the case went through different levels of courts. The United States government tried to have the case dismissed many times, but it continued. In 2018 the children won an important early victory when the US District Court allowed the case to proceed to trial, saying that the *plaintiffs* had a right to a climate capable of sustaining human life. Unfortunately, in 2020, the Court of Appeals dismissed the case, saying the courts did not have the power to order the government to do the things the children were asking it to do. However, the youth are not giving up. They have filed a motion against the federal government and the case continues to move through the courts. As a result of *Juliana v. United States*, thousands of youth, as well as members of the US Congress, religious and women's groups, businesses and many more, joined up to support action on climate change.

The court system can produce lasting change, but it works very slowly, and there is always the chance that a case won't be successful. However, there are many ways to create change and fight for the right to a healthy environment. People are taking to the streets, expressing themselves using art, science and more.

DEJUSTICIA

Colombian youth earn a win for the environment

In 2016 a group of Colombian youth between the ages of 7 and 26 took their government to the Supreme Court for not protecting the Amazon rainforest. The children and youth were from different parts of the country, and each wanted to live in a healthy environment.

At the time, José was an eighth-grade student and a member of the Ticuna Indigenous People who depend on the fish in the Amazon River. Candelaria was a fourth-grade student who lived on a farm with chickens, a native forest and springs of water. Candelaria suffered from asthma that often got worse when the temperature rose and the air filled with smoke when parts of the nearby forest burned. Aymara, eight years old at the time, often found her rural school classes canceled due to heavy rains that flooded the streets and blocked access to her school.

The young people argued that cutting down the Amazon threatens their future. When the forest isn't protected, neither are the fish they eat or the water they drink, and their homes are in danger of flooding. In 2018 they won their case! The court declared that the Amazon River ecosystem itself has the legal right to environmental protection. The decision showed young people that they can help make change, no matter their age. The court ordered the government of Colombia to create a plan that better protects the Amazon. The young people are still waiting for their government to act on the plan, and they continue to follow up to ensure that this will happen.

Four
Citizens Create Change

In August 2018, teen activist Greta Thunberg of Sweden sat alone outside the Swedish parliament building to protest climate change and the impact it will have on future generations. She stayed through the entire school day, handing out flyers to people who walked by. She returned the next day, but this time she wasn't alone. More and more people joined her, and in the following months her protest became known as the Fridays For Future movement. Since then she has inspired millions of people around the world to call for action against climate change. During the week of September 20–27, 2019, more than six million people marched in the streets of cities across the globe.

All these people used their democratic right to protest. Protests help bring people together about things they care about. The climate marches revealed that millions of people care about our planet's future. Protests can also help start conversations with the government about why things are the way they are and how we can start to make changes.

RONALD PATRICK/GETTY IMAGES

Many people say that Sweden is just a small country and it doesn't matter what we do, but I have learned you are never too small to make a difference.

—GRETA THUNBERG, speaking to the United Nations Climate Change Conference in December 2018 in Poland

67

Climate activist Greta Thunberg marches with thousands of students in Brussels in February 2019 to protest the government's climate policies. ALEXANDROS MICHAILIDIS/ SHUTTERSTOCK.COM

Protests can be big and messy. They stop traffic and interrupt everyday life. But the interruption is important because sometimes that's the only way to get people's attention.

STAND UP AND SPEAK OUT

For hundreds of years, people have protested against things they believed were wrong. Protesters have stood up to help protect people from harm at their place of work. They have protested women not having a vote. They've protested some people having to breathe dirty air so we all can have electricity. Each of these issues is about protecting human rights—the right to be equal, the right to be free and the right to live in a healthy environment.

Protests come in many forms. In 1988, César Chávez, the leader of a group of California farm workers, went on a 36-day hunger strike to raise awareness about dangerous pesticides that weren't safe for people or the environment. In southwestern British Columbia, community members from multiple Coast Salish nations built the Kwekwecnewtxw Watch House as part of their ongoing resistance to a pipeline. It's a traditional structure used to watch for enemies and protect their communities from danger.

One famous protest involved something that most people take for granted. Salt! The human body needs salt to function. But in India in 1930, people weren't allowed to collect salt. They had to buy it from the British rulers, who had made it so expensive that many Indian people couldn't afford it. Mahatma Gandhi decided he would go out and collect his own salt. He walked 240 miles (386 kilometers) in 24 days. Many people joined him along the way. When he arrived at the Arabian Sea, he picked up a handful of natural salt. This became known as the Salt March, and it wasn't just about salt. Gandhi's walk brought awareness that access to resources is a human right.

Citizens in Goa, India, peacefully strike on behalf of the planet on Friday, September 20, 2019. VIVEKCHUGH/SHUTTERSTOCK.COM

ACTIVISTS IN ACTION

The Sustainabiliteens

In December 2018, inspired by Greta Thunberg as well as Indigenous youth leaders, including Autumn Peltier and Ta'Kaiya Blaney, a group of teenagers from Vancouver, BC, joined together. Each of them believed something had to be done about the climate crisis. On September 27, 2019, they organized a strike for climate justice, expecting 10,000 people. More than 100,000 people arrived with handmade signs, ready to march.

The Sustainabiliteens believe that youth and children have the power to help adults imagine a more environmentally equal world. They suggest making connections with other people who care about the same issues. They say to start in your school or community. Build a team and dream of a more equal future.

I feel every individual has a right to know if their drinking water is safe.

—GITANJALI RAO,
who at age 11, inspired by the Flint, MI, water crisis, invented a device that can quickly test the water for lead contamination

In many countries, protests are peaceful, and the message is respected by the government. In other places, this is not the case. The right to protest is recognized by the Universal Declaration of Human Rights, but numerous governments have not respected or upheld this right. Many people speaking out for their environmental and human rights face danger. Berta Cáceres was a Lenca Indigenous woman from Honduras. For 20 years she fought for human rights and environmental justice. After leading her community in a protest against construction of a dam on a river sacred to the Lenca people, she was harassed and eventually assassinated for speaking out.

In Hong Kong, people protesting for democracy use umbrellas to symbolize resistance, shield them from tear gas and protect their identities.
LEWIS TSE PUI LUNG/SHUTTERSTOCK.COM

SPREAD THE WORD

Sometimes just one letter can make a big impression. When she was eight years old, Mari Copeny of Flint, Michigan, couldn't turn on the tap because the water was dangerous. Every drop of water she drank or used to brush her teeth had to come from a plastic bottle. Mari wrote a letter to then president Barack Obama and asked for his help, thinking the chances were low. Turned out he did read the letter! He went to Flint to meet her and learn more about the water issue, which helped raise awareness of the problem.

Although one letter can sometimes be effective, in other cases more attention is needed. **Social media** like Twitter or Facebook provide a place where anyone—citizens, government, companies, community groups—can express their views and share concerns. In 2016 a huge new oil pipeline was going to be built through the Standing Rock Sioux Tribe's

Volunteers from the American Red Cross deliver bottled water to homes in Flint, MI, in January 2016. At the time, the city water was too contaminated to drink.
SARAH RICE/GETTY IMAGES

YOU BE THE JUDGE

Protecting workers

Many of us use computers, buy food in plastic containers and wear clothes made by people on the other side of the planet. The raw materials for these products come from many sources, including ones that require children to work and live in unsafe, toxic conditions. Should the people who produce the products be guaranteed the right to safer, healthier working conditions? If you were the judge, what would you do?

land in North and South Dakota. Many people worried that the pipeline would pollute the region's water supply as well as damage sacred Indigenous sites. A group of Standing Rock youth decided to take action. The Standing Rock youth group, called ReZpect Our Water, used Twitter, Instagram, Facebook and YouTube to bring its message across the country and the world. The campaign became known by the *hashtag* #NoDAPL.

SONGS HAVE STRENGTH, PAINTINGS HAVE POWER

Many musicians inspire people to act for environmental rights. Xiuhtezcatl Martinez is a hip hop artist who became a climate activist at age six. His first album was released in 2014 and includes songs that bring awareness to environmental issues, including "Speak for the Trees" and "What the Frack." In 2019, at the age of 18, he performed for 350,000 people at the Friday for Future climate march in New York City.

Musician and former Earth Guardians youth director Xiuhtezcatl Martinez speaks onstage at WE Day California in April 2016.
MIKE WINDLE/GETTY IMAGES FOR WE DAY

When the power of music is paired with social media, great things can happen. Sofia Ashraf, a musician from Chennai, India, used social media to raise awareness of mercury poisoning at a factory near Kodaikanal in her home state of Tamil Nadu. More than 1,000 factory workers had fallen sick but weren't being given help, even though the mercury levels in the surrounding air, water and soil were higher than in other places, and the workers all had symptoms of mercury poisoning. Her music video attracted more than four million views on YouTube. Eventually the workers filed a lawsuit, and the company was forced to provide financial help for many people who had been poisoned.

Creating and displaying art is another powerful way to stand up for environmental rights. Marches and protests are great places to see how art can be used. When I see thousands of people carrying signs at a protest, I'm always astonished by how many people feel the same way yet find so many different ways to express that feeling.

Sofia Ashraf is a rapper from India whose music draws attention to corporations who fail to clean up industrial disasters. PHOTOGRAPHY BY ARJUN CHARANJIVA

In Dakota/Lakota we say "mni Wiconi." Water is life. Native American people know that water is the first medicine not just for us, but for all human beings living on this earth.

—ANNALEE RAIN YELLOW HAMMER, who at age 13, alongside other members of the Standing Rock Sioux Tribe, started a petition on change.org called Stop the Dakota Access Pipeline. It received 561,654 signatures.

Students in Munich create art for an upcoming Fridays For Future march to raise awareness of the climate crisis. What would your sign look like?
FOOTTOO/SHUTTERSTOCK.COM

In 2015, when Paris hosted the international climate change meeting, world leaders gathered in the city, along with climate activists, journalists and citizens. With so much attention on Paris, it was a great time for artists to make a statement about climate justice. One artist, Shepard Fairey, created a huge sculpture called *Earth Crisis* and hung it from the Eiffel Tower.

Art can come in so many forms. A Chinese artist who calls himself Nut Brother wanted to bring attention to air pollution. In 2016 he walked the streets of Beijing for 100 days, sucking up polluted air with an industrial vacuum cleaner. He mixed what he'd vacuumed from the air with clay to make bricks. His smog bricks were seen around the world on social media, bringing attention to the dangerous air that people in Beijing breathe.

SCIENCE CAN MAKE WAVES

When Stella Bowles was 11, she began to ask questions about why she wasn't allowed to swim in her local river in Nova Scotia. She learned it was because of straight pipes, a sewage-disposal system that flushed waste from toilets directly into the LaHave River. Even though they were illegal, there were 600 straight pipes emptying raw sewage into the river. Stella was upset by the straight pipes and wanted to know how polluted the river was because of all the poop. She decided to do her sixth-grade science project on the topic.

For Stella, science is way more than just a textbook at school. She believes kids can get out and take action at any age. BÉATRICE SCHULER-MOJON

Climate activist Licypriya Kangujam founded Child Movement, an India-based organization that aims to raise awareness about climate change to protect the planet's future.
LICYPRIYA KANGUJAM

Stella took samples of river water and tested for bacteria. She found contamination levels well above Canadian standards for swimming and boating. Stella decided she had to share her findings, as the river was a health hazard. She started a Facebook page and spread the word. She also put up a big sign by the river that said *This River Is Contaminated with Fecal Bacteria.* Stella's efforts got people's attention. Finally the Canadian government announced it would spend $15.7 million to clean up the LaHave River.

Young scientists are using their superpowers of observation to help solve environmental injustices. In communities around the world, people called **citizen scientists** collect scientific data such as water or soil samples to show where pollution is a problem. They then share their findings to try to make changes.

When she was eight years old, Licypriya Kangujam of India developed the SUKIFU (survival kit for the future) to bring awareness to air pollution in New Delhi. The kit is a potted house plant in a round glass backpack, with a tube that funnels fresh air from the backpack to the wearer's face mask. Licypriya hopes the device will attract attention and inspire change to reduce pollution.

MAKE YOUR VOICE HEARD

Across the globe, children and youth are finding ways to make their voices heard. In Kenya, before a national election in 2017, tens of thousands of children expressed their thoughts about what's important to them. They felt the government should focus on education, food security and building peace. In 2018 children at the Rosary Catholic Primary School in Birmingham, England, became activists for clean air after they discovered the pollution at their school was at illegal levels.

The government makes many decisions about how to protect our air, water and soil. Even if you aren't old enough to vote, you can still participate. You can write a letter to the editor of your local newspaper on an issue that's important to you. You can read the news or ask your parents about current events to learn more.

In Canada, since 2014, citizens of all ages have gone to their local governments to ask them to support environmental rights for their communities. Called the Blue Dot movement, the campaign aims to create awareness across the country about Canadians' right to clean air and water by working at the local level and then taking this community support to the next level of government. To date, 174 local government resolutions to support environmental rights, many brought forward by children and youth, have been passed.

It's a Fact

Stop, thief! Scientists are developing "chemical fingerprints" to track different toxic chemicals, with the hope of catching polluters red-handed.

SAMINA UMAR

Maryam and Nivaal Rehman

Maryam and Nivaal Rehman are identical twins who share a passion for environmental justice, equality for girls and women, journalism and filmmaking. Born in Pakistan, they moved to Canada when they were five years old, but they return often to visit their extended family. They have been activists since they were eight years old, volunteering in their local and global community to inspire people to take action.

In ninth grade they discovered that people in Canada don't have the right to a healthy environment. Immediately they started to use their energy and passion to help spread the word that not everyone in Canada has equal access to basic things like safe drinking water.

Maryam and Nivaal have some great advice for kids. Think about a cause you really care about and narrow it down. Climate justice is a big subject, but you might care about helping animals or protecting plants. The important thing is to focus on whatever it is that you care about. Then think about a talent that you have. "We combined our passion for the environment with filmmaking, and we made a documentary to raise awareness," said Maryam. "Be creative and you can really make a difference. Take the formula of Talent + Cause = Making Change!"

Frustrated by the lack of government action on climate change, American teenager Jamie Margolin gathered her friends and founded an organization called Zero Hour. It's now a national movement, with dozens of groups across the country. Supporters believe that action on climate change must also include creating a society that treats all citizens equally—no matter their culture, race or income. Through actions such as a climate summit in 2019 that trained over 350 youth in climate justice activism, they are demanding change for a more equal and sustainable future.

EVEN JUDGES NEED TO LEARN

I learned to read, write and do math in school. I learned about history and science. But looking back, I wish that I had learned about how we interact with our natural world. Where does our tap water go? What does air pollution do to our bodies? During the COVID-19 pandemic, when my son was home for schooling, we decided to make learning about the environment an everyday subject—it was his favorite!

Learning about the relationship between humans and the rest of the natural world is called ecological literacy. Ecological literacy can also include environmental justice. Let's Sprout is a program that was started by a group of young women in Nova Scotia who wanted to empower children and youth to create solutions to environmental problems in their community. Through workshops and leadership camps, elementary school students learn about environmental racism and **social justice**.

If we all learned more about how we impact the environment, how pollution affects our health and how environmental justice works, we could better speak up to make changes in our society. And it's not just kids and youth

YOU BE THE JUDGE

Banning diesel trucks

Most trucks still run on diesel, a fossil fuel similar to gasoline, only less expensive. People who drive these trucks are earning money to pay their bills and feed their families. Newer, more efficient trucks are expensive for people to buy. What if a city decides to make a new law in order to reduce pollution? They decide to ban older diesel trucks from entering the city. What will happen to the people who drive the trucks? If you were the judge, what would you do?

The walls of Let's Sprout's Creative Leadership Camp, where youth come to boost leadership skills, encourage meaningful connections and demand action.
SYDNEY MACLENNAN FOR LET'S SPROUT

who need to learn—lawyers and judges around the world continue to learn about environmental rights. The more they learn, the more they can make good decisions about environmental cases.

PASS ON GAS, SKIP TO SOLAR

Sometimes people would choose a job that lets them feed their families over having clean air. Other times people feel their right to freedom of choice should be ahead of all other rights. Climate justice asks even bigger questions about choice. In some countries, citizens have enjoyed driving cars and taking airplane trips across the planet for decades. All these trips were powered by burning fossil fuels. People in other countries might like those same opportunities.

The good news is that people are seeking new solutions to the problems with how we use and distribute resources. Instead of building more coal-fired power stations, some countries, including Peru, India and Bangladesh, are going straight

Just 18 percent of people on the planet have been on an airplane, and only about 3 percent of people go on one each year.
GUVENDEMIR/GETTY IMAGES

to solar or wind power. This gives people access to power without adding emissions. This seems like a win-win to me.

One of the questions popping up is whether cities should be for people or for cars. Cars pollute the air, and not everyone can afford them. Oslo, Norway, began limiting cars from its downtown in the 1970s. Car lanes and parking spots were turned into bike lanes, parks and benches. More cities have followed, such as Curitiba, Brazil, which decreased air pollution to the lowest levels in the country after increasing bus service and creating a car-free zone.

In 2020 San Francisco voted to ban personal cars from Market Street, the city's busiest street. It will be for people walking, biking or taking public transit. As more cities claim their streets for safe walking and bicycling, it will mean cleaner air for people and less impact on our climate.

Solar panels like these take energy from the sun and use it to generate electricity. Earth receives enough sunshine every day to potentially power all human activities! LEOPATRIZI/GETTY IMAGES

RIGHTS SPARK REAL CHANGE

Costa Rica, a small country in Central America, was once covered in rainforest. But by the 1980s, trees, animals and plants were disappearing. The government decided to act. In 1994 Costa Rica changed its constitution and gave every citizen the right to a healthy environment. People's basic human needs must be met without destroying resources for future generations. These were powerful words that led to powerful changes in the country.

Since then forests in Costa Rica have grown by more than 50 percent! Many people began to visit Costa Rica to see its forests, and that created more jobs for people living there. At the same time, the country was able to give more citizens better access to education. Costa Rica still faces challenges as its population grows. But it's wonderful to see that the right to a healthy environment can be a tool for protecting both people and the planet.

In 1999 the Constitutional Court of Costa Rica ruled that sea turtles must be protected as part of the right to a healthy and balanced ecosystem.
NATALIE11345/SHUTTERSTOCK.COM

COUNTRIES CAN COOPERATE

It's not easy, but countries have proven they can work together to accomplish great things! The ozone layer is a part of Earth's atmosphere. It acts like a big sunscreen for the planet. It keeps **UV radiation** from harming people, plants and animals. In the 1980s the ozone layer had thinned to the point that scientists were worried. Crops might fail. People might get sick from radiation. The problem was a type of chemical called a chlorofluorocarbon, or CFC. CFCs were used in all sorts of products, from fridges to hair spray. Scientists tested the air across the planet and found CFCs everywhere—even Antarctica, where the ozone layer was particularly thin. Newspapers began to call the thinning there "the ozone hole."

The ozone hole became front-page news and a global environmental emergency. Governments acted quickly. In 1987 many countries signed an international agreement to cut CFC emissions. More and more countries joined in the action. The best part was that they kept their promises. The ozone hole began to shrink and continues to do so today. The story of the ozone layer shows what's possible when countries join forces to protect human health.

When we view Earth from the perspective of space, it's easier to see how the environment is all connected: the atmosphere, the oceans and everything in between.
AARON FOSTER/GETTY IMAGES

WAYS TO CREATE CHANGE

Talk to your neighbors. Listen!

Learn all you can about the planet.

Make your voice count.

PUBLIC HEARING
Everyone Welcome!!

Use the power of science. Observe, collect and share data.

RALLY FOR THE ENVIRONMENT! 1:00 PM

YOUTH 4 CLIMATE

OUR PLANET OUR FUTURE!

Gather your friends to protest.

EACH OF US HAS SOMETHING TO GIVE!

Express yourself. Compose a song, draw, paint or sculpt.

YOU TOO CAN PLANT THE SEEDS OF CHANGE

In 1977 Professor Wangari Maathai founded the Green Belt Movement in Kenya in response to rural women's reports that streams were drying up and they had to walk farther and farther to find firewood for cooking. Professor Maathai helped women plant trees, which helped store rainwater, improve the soil and provide more firewood. To date, more than 51 million trees have been planted. Thousands of women have learned trades, such as beekeeping, that allow them to live a sustainable lifestyle and help the environment. In 2004 Wangari Maathai was the first African woman to win the Nobel Peace Prize. Since then many young people are following in her footsteps and mobilizing people to take small steps that result in big changes.

At age 12, Kehkashan Basu of the United Arab Emirates started the organization Green Hope Foundation to bring young people together to work for climate justice. Now, with groups working in six countries, Green Hope has already planted more than 15,000 trees. The groups also lead "environment academies," which are workshops to teach children about sustainable living and finding local solutions. No matter how small or how large, all efforts matter.

I hope this book has answered a few questions and sparked many more—I know it did for me! Environmental and climate justice requires cooperation from billions of people. That's a tall order, but the good news is each of us can make a difference, and small changes can create big results.

Back in chapter 2 I told you how in 1969 Lake Erie, one of the Great Lakes, was so polluted with toxic chemicals that it had been declared "dead." Accessing safe water from Lake Erie is still a huge issue for the 11 million people who live near the lake. But I was encouraged to read that in February

TOXIC TROUBLES

Radium is a *radioactive* chemical element discovered in 1898 by scientists Marie and Pierre Curie. Radium is shiny and even glows in the dark. Soldiers in World War I wore watches painted with radium to help them see the time in night battles. People started to use radium in everything from alarm clocks to cough syrup to water fountains. Radium was believed to have healing powers, so no one worried about negative health effects. Then a group of women who painted watch dials in a factory began to get sick and die. Eventually scientists proved that radium is toxic to humans, and people need protective gear when handling the substance.

Kehkashan Basu believes that, with their curiosity and enthusiasm, children and youth can create positive change for our environment.
KEHKASHAN BASU

"Clean lakes, not green lakes" is the message that residents of Toledo, OH, continue to spread as green algae blooms from industrial pollutants in Lake Erie make the water toxic to drink.
AARON P. BERNSTEIN/GETTY IMAGES

It's a Fact

On Monday, July 29, 2019, the citizens of Ethiopia set a new world record by planting 353 million new trees in one day!

2019 the people of Toledo, Ohio, voted to secure the legal right of Lake Erie to exist and flourish. Although the Lake Erie Bill of Rights was struck down in federal court in 2020, the idea that nature should have rights is gaining more attention, and this campaign got people talking. Now, similar campaigns are happening around the world, which is incredibly positive.

To me, one of the wonderful things about acknowledging our right to a healthy environment is that it reinforces the fact that all of us share the same Earth and everything is connected. When we start with the belief that all humans deserve clean air and water and healthy soil, we are starting from a place of respect——for people, animals and our planet. That means we can move forward with ideas that improve the quality of life for all living creatures. So let's get going! What change would you like to create?

Protected parks like this one on Mount Seymour in North Vancouver, BC, help people access nature and enjoy the benefits of hiking among the trees. PAMELAJOEMCFARLANE/GETTY IMAGES

GLOSSARY

acid rain—a form of air pollution. When fossil fuels such as coal or oil are burned, they release harmful gases into the air, combine with oxygen and water, then return to Earth as rain or snow.

activist—a person who campaigns for social change. Protests, art and social media are ways that an activist might work to create awareness and change.

anxiety—an emotion marked by feelings of tension, worried thoughts and physical changes like increased heart rate

atmosphere—the layer of gas that surrounds Earth, consisting mostly of nitrogen and oxygen

bacteria—tiny, single-celled organisms that are found everywhere around us. Also called microbes or germs

biodiversity—the variety of living things in a given place, including the plants, animals, bacteria and fungi

carbon dioxide—a colorless, odorless gas breathed out by animals and absorbed from the air by plants. It is also emitted by burning fossil fuels and is a greenhouse gas.

citizen scientists—members of the general public who volunteer their time to collect data relating to the natural world (i.e., counting birds, collecting water samples) in collaboration with professional scientists

civil rights movement—a decades-long struggle for equal rights for Black Americans

climate—the average weather conditions of a place or region

climate change—a long-term shift in global and regional weather and climate patterns caused by increased burning of fossil fuels. This includes the rise in global temperatures from the mid- to late-1900s to today.

climate justice—the fair treatment of all people with regard to policies and projects that address climate change and the systems that create it. Climate justice acknowledges that the impacts of climate change are not shared fairly.

climate migrants—people who are forced to leave their home region or country due to sudden or long-term changes in their environment—for example, a drought that threatens their ability to grow food or access water

constitution—a set of written laws that determine how a country operates and its overall values. The constitution also outlines the powers of the government and the rights its citizens are guaranteed.

contamination—the presence of something dangerous or impure. Food, air and water can be contaminated by hazardous substances or chemicals.

democracy—a form of government in which citizens can take part in how the government is run by voting for a leader and/or a representative. The word comes from two Greek words that mean "rule by the people."

discrimination—unfair treatment of a person or a group of people based on their gender, religion, nationality, culture, ability, race or personal traits such as age or appearance

drought—a long period of low rainfall, which leads to a shortage of water and to crop damage

emissions—substances released into the air, such as car exhaust or greenhouse gases from power plants and factories

environmental justice—the fair treatment and inclusion of all people with respect to developing and enforcing environmental laws and policies

environmental racism—exposing communities of people with low income or of visible minorities to more environmental hazards (such as toxic waste or pollution) than other groups are exposed to—for example, placing polluting industries in or near these communities or not cleaning up existing toxic sites

fossil fuels—materials that are formed from decaying plants and animals that were converted to oil, coal or natural gas by heat and pressure in Earth's crust over hundreds of millions of years

greenhouse gases—gases in Earth's atmosphere (such as carbon dioxide and methane) that trap heat and contribute to global warming

habitat—the natural home or environment of an animal, plant or other organism

hashtag—a word, phrase or sentence that starts with the hash sign (#). It is used on social media, especially Twitter, to identify messages on a specific topic.

ice age—a period of time when thick ice sheets called glaciers cover huge areas of the Earth. An ice age may last for millions of years. The last ice age was during the time of the woolly mammoths.

Industrial Revolution—beginning around the mid-1700s in England, the Industrial Revolution was a shift from making things by hand in shops and homes to using machines powered by the steam engine in larger factories. Many people moved from smaller villages and a life of farming to big cities to find work in the factories.

industrial waste—unused material or waste, such as scrap metal, oil or chemicals, that is produced by an industrial workplace, such as a factory, mill or mine. Industrial waste may be solid, liquid or a gas and can pollute the air, water or soil.

LGBTQ+—stands for lesbian, gay, bisexual, transgender and queer. The + indicates the intent to be inclusive of all the identities that make up this diverse community.

Paleolithic period—a time in history when humans began using chipped stone tools; also called the Old Stone Age, which started about 2.4 million years ago and lasted until about 10,000 BCE

parasites—living things, such as fleas, worms and fungi, that live on or inside other living things. Parasites take food from them and often cause harm, such as disease.

particulate matter (PM)—tiny particles of solid or liquid material that, when released into the atmosphere, can make the air we breathe dirty. They are linked to diseases like lung cancer.

persecution—the cruel and unfair treatment of a person or a group of people, often based on their religion, gender identity, race or ethnicity

pesticides—chemical substances that are meant to control pests, including weeds and insects

phthalates—a group of chemicals used to make plastics more flexible. They are used today in hundreds of products, including food packaging, shampoos, hair spray and garden hoses

plaintiffs—a group of people who bring a legal case to court against another person, group or organization

pollution—the presence or introduction into the environment of a harmful or poisonous substance. These harmful materials are called pollutants.

radioactive—having or producing energy in the form of radiation. Some elements, including uranium and radium, are made up of unstable atoms, which means they change over time and release energy, which we call radiation.

settlers—people who arrive uninvited to a new place from another country or region to live there and use the land, such as the Europeans who came to North America

social justice—the fair treatment of all people with regard to access to resources and programs that promote their health and well-being, such as medical care, housing and education

social media—interactive technologies for computers, phones and tablets that allow people to people create and share ideas, photos and other information as well as create virtual communities. Examples are Twitter and YouTube.

soil—a mix of minerals, gases, water, organic matter and dead and living organisms. It provides essential nutrients to plants and crops.

supreme court—the highest court of law in a country

sustainable—able to meet the needs of people and the environment now and in the future. Using natural resources in a sustainable way means not depleting them or damaging the environment.

temperature inversion—an increase in air temperature as altitude increases, rather than the other way around, so that the air closest to the ground is colder than the air above. When a warm mass of air moves over a cold mass of air, it may trap the cold air below, along with any existing fog or pollution.

toxic—poisonous or harmful to humans, animals or plants

United Nations—an organization of 193 countries that aims to maintain international peace, security and cooperation

UV radiation—ultraviolet radiation, which refers to the invisible rays that are part of the energy that comes from the sun. They can burn the skin and cause skin cancer.

values—the basic principles and beliefs that guide your actions and help you decide what is right and wrong and what's important in life

Garbage floats in the ocean near Greenland, just one piece of the billions of pounds of plastic in our oceans. Sea turtles and other marine animals can mistake floating plastic garbage for food.
POSTERIORI/GETTY IMAGES

RESOURCES

Books

Bowles, Stella, with Anne Laurel Carter. *My River: Cleaning up the LaHave River.* Halifax, NS: Formac Publishing, 2018.

Clendenan, Megan, and Kim Ryall Woolcock. *Design Like Nature: Biomimicry for a Healthy Planet.* Victoria, BC: Orca Book Publishers, 2021.

Heos, Bridget. *It's Getting Hot in Here: The Past, Present, and Future of Climate Change.* New York, NY: Houghton Mifflin Harcourt, 2016.

McLaughlin, Danielle S. *That's Not Fair: Getting to Know Your Rights and Freedoms.* Toronto, ON: Kids Can Press, Citizen Kid Imprint, 2016.

Oposa, Antonio, Jr. *Shooting Stars and Dancing Fish: A Walk to the World We Want.* Bantayan Island, Cebu, the Philippines: School of the SEA, 2017.

Rae, Rowena. *Chemical World: Science in Our Daily Lives.* Victoria, BC: Orca Book Publishers, 2020.

Rao, Anuradha. *One Earth: People of Color Protecting Our Planet.* Victoria, BC: Orca Book Publishers, 2020.

Rippon, Jo. *Rise Up! The Art of Protest.* Watertown, MA: Charlesbridge, 2020.

Smith, David J. *If the World Were a Village: A Book about the World's People,* 2nd ed. Toronto, ON: Kids Can Press, 2011.

Stevenson, Robin. *Kid Activists: True Tales of Childhood from Champions of Change.* Philadelphia, PA: Quirk Books, 2019.

Tate, Nikki. *Better Together: Creating Community in an Uncertain World.* Victoria, BC: Orca Book Publishers, 2018.

Websites

Blue Dot Movement: bluedot.ca

Earth Guardians: earthguardians.org

Ecojustice: ecojustice.ca

Footprint Network: footprintnetwork.org

Fridays For Future: fridaysforfuture.org

Green Hope Foundation: greenhopefoundation.com

International Children's Peace Prize: kidsrights.org/
     advocacy/international-childrens-peace-prize

Our Children's Trust: ourchildrenstrust.org

The Story of Stuff Project: storyofstuff.org

United Nations Declaration of Human Rights:
     un.org/en/universal-declaration-human-rights

World With MNR (Maryam and Nivaal Rehman, activists):
     theworldwithmnr.com

Zero Hour: thisiszerohour.org

Rays of sun filter through smoky forest in August 2020 in California. A fire known as the Apple Fire forced thousands to flee their homes before flames burned 12,000 acres (4,856 hectares) in one afternoon near the San Bernardino Mountains.
DAVID MCNEW/GETTY IMAGES

An iceberg floats by in Jökulsárlón, a glacial lake in Vatnajökull National Park, Iceland. The lake has quadrupled in size since the 1970s, after icebergs began to calve off the glacier. FRANCKREPORTER/GETTY IMAGES

ACKNOWLEDGMENTS

A huge thank-you to everyone who let me interview them for this book. I learned so much from each of you! A special shout-out to Maryam and Nivaal Rehman, Stella and Andrea Bowles, the Sustainabiliteens, Ingrid Waldron, Margot Venton and Peter Wood. Many others wrote me long and helpful emails. I'm also incredibly grateful to Dr. Stepan Wood, director of the Centre for Law and the Environment at the University of British Columbia, who read the manuscript, pointed out confusing and misleading passages, and connected me with environmental lawyer Antonio Oposa Jr., who graciously offered resources for this project. I'm also thankful for the informative and inspiring books on environmental rights by Dr. David Boyd. Any mistakes in the text are mine.

Thank you to all at Orca Book Publishers for producing such amazing books and not shying away from the tough topics that matter. Thanks in particular to my editor, Kirstie Hudson, for your keen eye for detail and ability to ask the right questions, and copyeditor Vivian Sinclair, who helped make the book shine. I'm so grateful for Julie McLaughlin's illustrations, which show so beautifully how we are all connected to the earth, air and water.

Many wonderful readers offered their time and wisdom, in particular Kim Woolcock and Nina Giuliani. Thanks to my family, Dave and Owen, who patiently listened to me talk incessantly about this topic for many months, read the rough drafts, offered great ideas and challenged me to ask even more questions.

INDEX

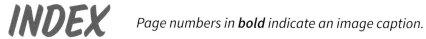

*Page numbers in **bold** indicate an image caption.*

DAVE CLENDENAN

MEGAN CLENDENAN has worked for women's rights, mental health and youth empowerment nonprofits as well as for an environmental law group, where she realized for the first time that the court system could be a way to help protect human health from pollution and toxic chemicals. She is the co-author of *Design Like Nature*, part of the Orca Footprints series, and the author of *Offbeat*, a novel for young readers in the Orca Limelights series. Megan lives in North Vancouver, British Columbia, with her family.

ORCA Think

Stay Curious!

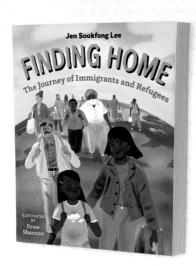

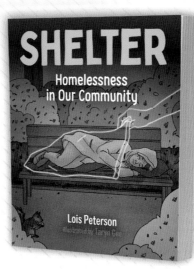

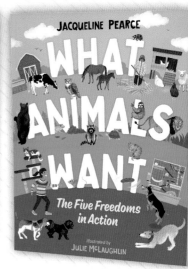

WHAT'S THE BIG IDEA?

The Orca Think series introduces us to the issues making headlines in the world today. It encourages us to question, connect and take action for a better future. With those tools we can all become better citizens. Now that's smart thinking!